ROADMAP

to

SUCCESS

TABLE OF CONTENTS

A Message from the Publisher

I've done a lot of driving in my life and one thing I have been smart enough to have is a dependable road map. If you don't have a good plan to get from where you are to where you want to go, you will get lost.

I've known many people who have started out in business and thought they had a good plan, but did not achieve the success they wanted. A major problem for many of these people was that they had not sought good advice from people who had achieved success. If you don't learn from the experience of others, you might achieve success but you will probably get there the hard way. You might get lost down many side roads before you find the right one.

Roadmap to Success, is a mini-seminar on how to plan for your success. The successful people in this book have the experience that will help you find what you need to create your road map to success. These perceptive businesspeople were fascinating as they unfolded their own personal road maps and told me about their various success journeys.

I invite you to set aside some quiet time and learn from these exceptional authors. I assure you that your time won't be wasted. It's not often that you can access such a large quantity of quality information that will either get you started or help you get further along on your road to success. This book is an investment in your future—your successful future!

Interviews Conducted by:
David E. Wright, President
Insight Publishing & International Speakers Network

ROADMAP to SUCCESS 1

An interview with...

Dr. Ken Blanchard

David E. Wright (Wright)

Few people have created a positive impact on the day-to-day management of people and companies more than Dr. Kenneth Blanchard. He is known around the world simply as Ken, a prominent, gregarious, sought-after author, speaker, and business consultant. Ken is universally characterized by friends, colleagues, and clients as one of the most insightful, powerful, and compassionate men in business today. Ken's impact as a writer is far-reaching. His phenomenal best-selling book, *The One Minute Manager*®, coauthored with Spencer Johnson, has sold more than thirteen million copies worldwide and has been translated into more than twenty-five languages. Ken is Chairman and "Chief Spiritual Officer" of the Ken Blanchard Companies. The organization's focus is to energize organizations around the world with customized training in bottom-line business strategies based on the simple, yet powerful principles inspired by Ken's best-selling books.

Dr. Blanchard, welcome to *Roadmap to Success*.

Dr. Ken Blanchard (Blanchard)

Well, it's nice to talk with you, David. It's good to be here.

Wright

I must tell you that preparing for your interview took quite a bit more time than usual. The scope of your life's work and your business, the Ken Blanchard Companies, would make for a dozen fascinating interviews.

Before we dive into the specifics of some of your projects and strategies, will you give our readers a brief synopsis of your life—how you came to be the Ken Blanchard we all know and respect?

Blanchard

Well, I'll tell you, David, I think life is what you do when you are planning on doing something else. I think that was John Lennon's line. I never intended to do what I have been doing. In fact, all my professors in college told me that I couldn't write. I wanted to do college work, which I did, and they said, "You had better be an administrator." So I decided I was going to be a Dean of Students. I got provisionally accepted into my master's degree program and then provisionally accepted at Cornell because I never could take any of those standardized tests.

I took the college boards four times and finally got 502 in English. I don't have a test-taking mind. I ended up in a university in Athens, Ohio, in 1966 as an Administrative Assistant to the Dean of the Business School. When I got there he said, "Ken, I want you to teach a course. I want all my deans to teach." I had never thought about teaching because they said I couldn't write, and teachers had to publish. He put me in the manager's department.

I've taken enough bad courses in my day and I wasn't going to teach one. I really prepared and had a wonderful time with the students. I was chosen as one of the top ten teachers on the campus coming out of the chute!

I just had a marvelous time. A colleague by the name of Paul Hersey was chairman of the Management Department. He wasn't very friendly to me initially because the Dean had led me to his department, but I heard he was a great teacher. He taught Organizational Behavior and Leadership. So I said, "Can I sit in on your course next semester?"

"Nobody audits my courses," he said. "If you want to take it for credit, you're welcome."

I couldn't believe it. I had a doctoral degree and he wanted me to take his course for credit—so I signed up.

The registrar didn't know what to do with me because I already had a doctorate, but I wrote the papers and took the course, and it was great.

In June 1967, Hersey came into my office and said, "Ken, I've been teaching in this field for ten years. I think I'm better than anybody, but I can't write. I'm a nervous wreck, and I'd love to write a textbook with somebody. Would you write one with me?"

I said, "We ought to be a great team. You can't write and I'm not supposed to be able to, so let's do it!"

Thus began this great career of writing and teaching. We wrote a textbook called *Management of Organizational Behavior: Utilizing Human Resources*. It came out in its eighth edition October 3, 2000, and the ninth edition was published September 3, 2007. It has sold more than any other textbook in that area over the years. It's been over forty years since that book first came out.

I quit my administrative job, became a professor, and ended up working my way up the ranks. I got a sabbatical leave and went to California for one year twenty-five years ago. I ended up meeting Spencer Johnson at a cocktail party. He wrote children's books—a wonderful series called *Value Tales*® *for*

Kids. He also wrote *The Value of Courage: The Story of Jackie Robinson* and *The Value of Believing In Yourself: The Story of Louis Pasteur.*

My wife, Margie, met him first and said, "You guys ought to write a children's book for managers because they won't read anything else." That was my introduction to Spencer. So, *The One Minute Manager* was really a kid's book for big people. That is a long way from saying that my career was well planned.

Wright

Ken, what and/or who were your early influences in the areas of business, leadership, and success? In other words, who shaped you in your early years?

Blanchard

My father had a great impact on me. He was retired as an admiral in the Navy and had a wonderful philosophy. I remember when I was elected as president of the seventh grade, and I came home all pumped up. My father said, "Son, it's great that you're the president of the seventh grade, but now that you have that leadership position, don't ever use it." He said, "Great leaders are followed because people respect them and like them, not because they have power." That was a wonderful lesson for me early on. He was just a great model for me. I got a lot from him.

Then I had this wonderful opportunity in the mid-1980s to write a book with Norman Vincent Peale. He wrote *The Power of Positive Thinking.* I met him when he was eighty-six years old; we were asked to write a book on ethics together, *The Power of Ethical Management: Integrity Pays, You Don't Have to Cheat to Win.* It didn't matter what we were writing together; I learned so much from him. He just built from the positive things I learned from my mother.

My mother said that when I was born I laughed before I cried, I danced before I walked, and I smiled before I frowned. So that, as well as Norman Vincent Peale, really impacted me as I focused on what I could do to train

4

leaders. How do you make them positive? How do you make them realize that it's not about them, it's about who they are serving? It's not about their position—it's about what they can do to help other people win.

So, I'd say my mother and father, then Norman Vincent Peale. All had a tremendous impact on me.

Wright

I can imagine. I read a summary of your undergraduate and graduate degrees. I assumed you studied Business Administration, marketing management, and related courses. Instead, at Cornell you studied Government and Philosophy. You received your master's from Colgate in Sociology and Counseling and your PhD from Cornell in Educational Administration and Leadership. Why did you choose this course of study? How has it affected your writing and consulting?

Blanchard

Well, again, it wasn't really well planned out. I originally went to Colgate to get a master's degree in Education because I was going to be a Dean of Students over men. I had been a Government major, and I was a Government major because it was the best department at Cornell in the Liberal Arts School. It was exciting. We would study what the people were doing at the league of governments. And then, the Philosophy Department was great. I just loved the philosophical arguments. I wasn't a great student in terms of getting grades, but I'm a total learner. I would sit there and listen, and I would really soak it in.

When I went over to Colgate and got into the education courses, they were awful. They were boring. The second week, I was sitting at the bar at the Colgate Inn saying, "I can't believe I've been here two years for this." This is just the way the Lord works: Sitting next to me in the bar was a young sociology professor who had just gotten his PhD at Illinois. He was staying at the Inn. I was moaning and groaning about what I was doing, and he said, "Why don't you come and major with me in sociology? It's really exciting."

"I can do that?" I asked.

He said, "Yes."

I knew they would probably let me do whatever I wanted the first week. Suddenly, I switched out of Education and went with Warren Ramshaw. He had a tremendous impact on me. He retired some years ago as the leading professor at Colgate in the Arts and Sciences, and got me interested in leadership and organizations. That's why I got a master's in Sociology.

The reason I went into educational administration and leadership? It was a doctoral program I could get into because I knew the guy heading up the program. He said, "The greatest thing about Cornell is that you will be in the School of Education. It's not very big, so you don't have to take many education courses, and you can take stuff all over the place."

There was a marvelous man by the name of Don McCarty who eventually became the Dean of the School of Education, Wisconsin. He had an impact on my life; but I was always just searching around.

My mission statement is: to be a loving teacher and example of simple truths that help myself and others to awaken the presence of God in our lives. The reason I mention "God" is that I believe the biggest addiction in the world is the human ego; but I'm really into simple truth. I used to tell people I was trying to get the B.S. out of the behavioral sciences.

Wright

I can't help but think, when you mentioned your father, that he just bottom-lined it for you about leadership.

Blanchard

Yes.

Wright

A man named Paul Myers, in Texas, years and years ago when I went to a conference down there, said, "David, if you think you're a leader and you look around, and no one is following you, you're just out for a walk."

Blanchard

Well, you'd get a kick out of this—I'm just reaching over to pick up a picture of Paul Myers on my desk. He's a good friend, and he's a part of our Center for FaithWalk Leadership where we're trying to challenge and equip people to lead like Jesus. It's non-profit. I tell people I'm not an evangelist because we've got enough trouble with the Christians we have. We don't need any more new ones. But, this is a picture of Paul on top of a mountain. Then there's another picture below that of him under the sea with stingrays. It says, "Attitude is everything. Whether you're on the top of the mountain or the bottom of the sea, true happiness is achieved by accepting God's promises, and by having a biblically positive frame of mind. Your attitude is everything." Isn't that something?

Wright

He's a fine, fine man. He helped me tremendously. In keeping with the theme of our book, *Roadmap for Success,* I wanted to get a sense from you about your own success journey. Many people know you best from *The One Minute Manager* books you coauthored with Spencer Johnson. Would you consider these books as a high water mark for you or have you defined success for yourself in different terms?

Blanchard

Well, you know, *The One Minute Manager* was an absurdly successful book so quickly that I found I couldn't take credit for it. That was when I really got on my own spiritual journey and started to try to find out what the real meaning of life and success was.

That's been a wonderful journey for me because I think, David, the problem with most people is they think their self-worth is a function of their performance plus the opinion of others. The minute you think that is what your self-worth is, every day your self-worth is up for grabs because your performance is going to fluctuate on a day-to-day basis. People are fickle.

Their opinions are going to go up and down. You need to ground your self-worth in the unconditional love that God has ready for us, and that really grew out of the unbelievable success of *The One Minute Manager.*

When I started to realize where all that came from, that's how I got involved in this ministry that I mentioned. Paul Myers is a part of it. As I started to read the Bible, I realized that everything I've ever written about, or taught, Jesus did. You know, He did it with the twelve incompetent guys He "hired." The only guy with much education was Judas, and he was His only turnover problem.

Wright

Right.

Blanchard

This is a really interesting thing. What I see in people is not only do they think their self-worth is a function of their performance plus the opinion of others, but they measure their success on the amount of accumulation of wealth, on recognition, power, and status. I think those are nice success items. There's nothing wrong with those, as long as you don't define your life by that.

What I think you need to focus on rather than success is what Bob Buford, in his book *Halftime,* calls "significance"—moving from success to significance. I think the opposite of accumulation of wealth is generosity.

I wrote a book called *The Generosity Factor* with Truett Cathy, who is the founder of Chick-fil-A. He is one of the most generous men I've ever met in my life. I thought we needed to have a model of generosity. It's not only your *treasure,* but it's your *time* and *talent.* Truett and I added *touch* as a fourth one.

The opposite of recognition is service. I think you become an adult when you realize you're here to serve rather than to be served.

Finally, the opposite of power and status is loving relationships. Take Mother Teresa as an example—she couldn't have cared less about recognition, power, and status because she was focused on generosity, service, and loving relationships; but she got all of that earthly stuff. If you focus on the earthly, such as money, recognition, and power, you're never going to get to significance. But if you focus on significance, you'll be amazed at how much success can come your way.

Wright

I spoke with Truett Cathy recently and was impressed by what a down-to-earth, good man he seems to be. When you start talking about him closing his restaurants on Sunday, all of my friends—when they found out I had talked to him—said, "Boy, he must be a great Christian man, but he's rich." I told them, "Well, to put his faith into perspective, by closing on Sunday it costs him $500 million a year."

He lives his faith, doesn't he?

Blanchard

Absolutely, but he still outsells everybody else.

Wright

That's right.

Blanchard

According to their January 25, 2007, press release, Chick-fil-A was the nation's second-largest quick-service chicken restaurant chain in sales at that time. Its business performance marks the thirty-ninth consecutive year the chain has enjoyed a system-wide sales gain—a streak the company has sustained since opening its first chain restaurant in 1967.

Wright

The simplest market scheme, I told him, tripped me up. I walked by his first Chick-fil-A I had ever seen, and some girl came out with chicken stuck on toothpicks and handed me one; I just grabbed it and ate it; it's history from there on.

Blanchard

Yes, I think so. It's really special. It is so important that people understand generosity, service, and loving relationships because too many people are running around like a bunch of peacocks. You even see pastors who measure their success by how many are in their congregation; authors by how many books they have sold; businesspeople by what their profit margin is—how good sales are. The reality is, that's all well and good, but I think what you need to focus on is the other. I think if business did that more and we got Wall Street off our backs with all the short-term evaluation, we'd be a lot better off.

Wright

Absolutely. There seems to be a clear theme that winds through many of your books that has to do with success in business and organizations—how people are treated by management and how they feel about their value to a company. Is this an accurate observation? If so, can you elaborate on it?

Blanchard

Yes, it's a very accurate observation. See, I think the profit is the applause you get for taking care of your customers and creating a motivating environment for your people. Very often people think that business is only about the bottom line. But no, that happens to be the result of creating raving fan customers, which I've described with Sheldon Bowles in our book, *Raving Fans*. Customers want to brag about you, if you create an environment where people can be gung-ho and committed. You've got to take care of your customers and your people, and then your cash register is going to go ka-ching, and you can make some big bucks.

Wright

I noticed that your professional title with the Ken Blanchard Companies is somewhat unique—"Chairman and Chief Spiritual Officer." What does your title mean to you personally and to your company? How does it affect the books you choose to write?

Blanchard

I remember having lunch with Max DuPree one time. The legendary Chairman of Herman Miller, Max wrote a wonderful book called *Leadership Is an Art.*

"What's your job?" I asked him.

He said, "I basically work in the vision area."

"Well, what do you do?" I asked.

"I'm like a third-grade teacher," he replied. "I say our vision and values over, and over, and over again until people get it right, right, right."

I decided from that, I was going to become the Chief Spiritual Officer, which means I would be working in the vision, values, and energy part of our business. I ended up leaving a morning message every day for everybody in our company. We have twenty-eight international offices around the world.

I leave a voice mail every morning, and I do three things on that as Chief Spiritual Officer: One, people tell me who we need to pray for. Two, people tell me who we need to praise—our unsung heroes and people like that. And then three, I leave an inspirational morning message. I really am the cheerleader—the Energizer Bunny—in our company. I'm the reminder of why we're here and what we're trying to do.

We think that our business in the Ken Blanchard Companies is to help people lead at a higher level, and to help individuals and organizations. Our mission statement is to unleash the power and potential of people and organizations for the common good. So if we are going to do that, we've really got to believe in that.

I'm working on getting more Chief Spiritual Officers around the country. I think it's a great title and we should get more of them.

Wright

So those people for whom you pray, where do you get the names?

Blanchard

The people in the company tell me who needs help, whether it's a spouse who is sick or kids who are sick or if they are worried about something. We've got over five years of data about the power of prayer, which is pretty important.

One morning, my inspirational message was about my wife and five members of our company who walked sixty miles one weekend—twenty miles a day for three days—to raise money for breast cancer research.

It was amazing. I went down and waved them all in as they came. They had a ceremony; they had raised $7.6 million. There were over three thousand people walking. A lot of the walkers were dressed in pink—they were cancer victors—people who had overcome it. There were even men walking with pictures of their wives who had died from breast cancer. I thought it was incredible.

There wasn't one mention about it in the major San Diego papers. I said, "Isn't that just something." We have to be an island of positive influence because all you see in the paper today is about celebrities and their bad behavior. Here you have all these thousands of people out there walking and trying to make a difference, and nobody thinks it's news.

So every morning I pump people up about what life's about, about what's going on. That's what my Chief Spiritual Officer job is about.

Wright

I had the pleasure of reading one of your releases, *The Leadership Pill.*

Blanchard

Yes.

Wright

I must admit that my first thought was how short the book was. I wondered if I was going to get my money's worth, which by the way, I most certainly did. Many of your books are brief and based on a fictitious story. Most business books in the market today are hundreds of pages in length and are read almost like a textbook.

Will you talk a little bit about why you write these short books, and about the premise of *The Leadership Pill?*

Blanchard

I really developed my relationship with Spencer Johnson when we wrote *The One Minute Manager.* As you know, he wrote, *Who Moved My Cheese,* which was a phenomenal success. He wrote children's books and is quite a storyteller.

Jesus taught by parables, which were short stories.

My favorite books are *Jonathan Livingston Seagull* and *The Little Prince.* Og Mandino, author of seventeen books, was the greatest of them all.

I started writing parables because people can get into the story and learn the contents of the story, and they don't bring their judgmental hats into reading. You write a regular book and they'll say, "Well, where did you get the research?" They get into that judgmental side. Our books get them emotionally involved and they learn.

The Leadership Pill is a fun story about a pharmaceutical company that thinks they have discovered the secret to leadership, and they can put the ingredients in a pill. When they announce it, the country goes crazy because everybody knows we need more effective leaders. When they release it, it outsells Viagra.

The founders of the company start selling off stock and they call them Pillionaires. But along comes this guy who calls himself "the effective manager," and he challenges them to a no-pill challenge. If they identify two non-performing groups, he'll take on one and let somebody on the pill take another one, and he guarantees he will outperform that person by the end of the year. They agree, but of course they give him a drug test every week to make sure he's not sneaking pills on the side.

I wrote the book with Marc Muchnick, who is a young guy in his early thirties. We did a major study of what this interesting "Y" generation—the young people of today—want from leaders, and this is a secret blend that this effective manager uses. When you think about it, David, it is really powerful in terms of what people want from a leader.

Number one, they want integrity. A lot of people have talked about that in the past, but these young people will walk if they see people say one thing and do another. A lot of us walk to the bathroom and out into the halls to talk about it. But these people will quit. They don't want somebody to say something and not do it.

The second thing they want is a partnership relationship. They hate superior/subordinate. I mean, what awful terms those are. You know, the "head" of the department and the hired "hands"—you don't even give them a head. "What do I do? I'm in supervision. I see things a lot clearer than these stupid idiots." They want to be treated as partners; if they can get a financial partnership, great. If they can't, they really want a minimum of a psychological partnership where they can bring their brains to work and make decisions.

Then finally, they want affirmation. They not only want to be caught doing things right, but they want to be affirmed for who they are. They want to be known as individual people, not as numbers.

So those are the three ingredients that this effective manager uses. They are wonderful values when you think about them.

Rank-order values for any organization is number one, integrity. In our company we call it ethics. It is our number one value. The number two value is partnership. In our company we call it relationships. Number three is affirmation—being affirmed as a human being. I think that ties into relationships, too. They are wonderful values that can drive behavior in a great way.

Wright

I believe most people in today's business culture would agree that success in business has everything to do with successful leadership. In *The Leadership Pill,* you present a simple but profound premise; that leadership is not something you do to people; it's something you do *with* them. At face value, that seems incredibly obvious. But you must have found in your research and observations that leaders in today's culture do not get this. Would you speak to that issue?

Blanchard

Yes. I think what often happens in this is the human ego. There are too many leaders out there who are self-serving. They're not leaders who have service in mind. They think the sheep are there for the benefit of the shepherd. All the power, money, fame, and recognition move up the hierarchy. They forget that the real action in business is not up the hierarchy—it's in the one-to-one, moment-to-moment interactions that your frontline people have with your customers. It's how the phone is answered. It's how problems are dealt with and those kinds of things. If you don't think that you're doing leadership *with* them—rather, you're doing it *to* them—after a while they won't take care of your customers.

I was at a store once (not Nordstrom's, where I normally would go) and I thought of something I had to share with my wife, Margie. I asked the guy behind the counter in Men's Wear, "May I use your phone?"

He said, "No!"

"You're kidding me," I said. "I can always use the phone at Nordstrom's."

"Look, buddy," he said, "they won't let *me* use the phone here. Why should I let you use the phone?"

That is an example of leadership that's done *to* employees, not *with* them. People want a partnership. People want to be involved in a way that really makes a difference.

Wright

Dr. Blanchard, the time has flown by and there are so many more questions I'd like to ask you. In closing, would you mind sharing with our readers some thoughts on success? If you were mentoring a small group of men and women, and one of their central goals was to become successful, what kind of advice would you give them?

Blanchard

Well, I would first of all say, "What are you focused on?" If you are focused on success as being, as I said earlier, accumulation of money, recognition, power, or status, I think you've got the wrong target. What you need to really be focused on is how you can be generous in the use of your time and your talent and your treasure and touch. How can you serve people rather than be served? How can you develop caring, loving relationships with people? My sense is if you will focus on those things, success in the traditional sense will come to you. But if you go out and say, "Man, I'm going to make a fortune, and I'm going to do this," and have that kind of attitude, you might get some of those numbers. I think you become an adult, however, when you realize you are here to give rather than to get. You're here to serve, not to be served. I would just say to people, "Life is such a very special occasion. Don't miss it by aiming at a target that bypasses other people, because we're really here to serve each other."

Wright

Well, what an enlightening conversation, Dr. Blanchard. I really want you to know how much I appreciate all the time you've taken with me for this interview. I know that our readers will learn from this, and I really appreciate your being with us today.

Blanchard

Well, thank you so much, David. I really enjoyed my time with you. You've asked some great questions that made me think, and I hope my answers are helpful to other people because as I say, life is a special occasion.

Wright

Today we have been talking with Dr. Ken Blanchard. He is coauthor of the phenomenal best-selling book, *The One Minute Manager*. The fact that he's the Chief Spiritual Officer of his company should make us all think about how we are leading our companies and leading our families and leading anything, whether it is in church or civic organizations. I know I will.

Thank you so much, Dr. Blanchard, for being with us today.

Blanchard

Good to be with you, David.

ABOUT THE AUTHOR

Few people have created more of a positive impact on the day-to-day management of people and companies than Dr. Kenneth Blanchard, who is known around the world simply as "Ken."

When Ken speaks, he speaks from the heart with warmth and humor. His unique gift is to speak to an audience and communicate with each individual as if they were alone and talking one-on-one. He is a polished storyteller with a knack for making the seemingly complex easy to understand.

Ken has been a guest on a number of national television programs, including *Good Morning America* and *The Today Show*. He has been featured in *Time, People, U.S. News & World Report*, and a host of other popular publications.

He earned his bachelor's degree in Government and Philosophy from Cornell University, his master's degree in Sociology and Counseling from Colgate University, and his PhD in Educational Administration and Leadership from Cornell University.

Dr. Ken Blanchard
The Ken Blanchard Companies
125 State Place
Escondido, California 92029
800.728.6000
Fax: 760.489.8407
www.kenblanchard.com

ROADMAP *to* SUCCESS 2

An interview with...

Bill Bachrach

David Wright (Wright)

Today we are talking with Bill Bachrach, CSP. Bill is Founder and Chairman of Bachrach & Associates, Inc. (BAI). BAI is a well-known training and development company for financial professionals. Established in 1988, BAI has a full complement of training, coaching, and support services to help financial professionals implement Values-Based Financial Planning™. In addition, Bill is a best-selling author and an accomplished keynote speaker.

Bill, what is a Success Road Map®?

Bill Bachrach (Bachrach)

I am so thrilled that you are about to discover the power of the Success Road Map!

Like most of us who care about being successful, chances are pretty high that when you look in the mirror you see two people: the person you are and the person you're capable of being. The purpose of this Success Road Map chapter is to help you become more of the person you are capable of being. You will discover how answering the important questions that drive this fun tool can help you have your best year ever and enhance your life forever. Your Success Road Map can be the launching pad for you to experience more success and happiness than you might have previously imagined possible.

Thousands of people have benefitted from having experienced the Success Road Map process, and I hope it has a similar positive impact for you.

The Success Road Map is a big, colorful, visual tool that contains the most important information that personally inspires—*you*. See the diagram below for perspective on how each element of the Success Road Map fits together. At the end of this chapter there are instructions for ordering a complimentary Success Road Map.

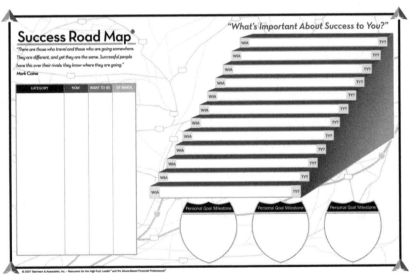

For most people, their Success Road Map serves at least two critical purposes:

1. It provides the framework from which you do all of your business and life planning.

2. It serves as a powerful tool to help you stay on track and get back on track when the inevitable crush of too much to do and not enough time drives you off your plan.

Let's be honest with ourselves; most of us would be much more successful if we would just *consistently* do what we already know needs to be done.

Peter Vidmar was the captain of the 1984, gold-medal-winning men's Olympic gymnastics team, and the Olympian who scored a perfect ten on the pommel horse to capture gold in that event. Since then he has enjoyed a very successful career as a motivational speaker and author. He says, "To be a champion you only have to do two things: work out when you feel like it, and work out when you *don't* feel like it."

We all do what needs to be done on the days when we feel like it. Where do we find the right inspiration and that little nudge we might need on the days when we *don't* feel like it? The answers are on your Success Road Map. It serves as a constant reminder of the values and goals that drive *you*. It helps you stay focused on the action required to bridge the gap between where you are now and where you want to be so you achieve your goals for the reasons that are important to you. People often describe their Success Road Map as a simple tool that provides clarity, focus, and inspiration to help them maintain the perspective that keeps their lives in balance.

Wright

Who should have a Success Road Map?

Bachrach

Self-employed professionals, business owners, entrepreneurs, and everyone who prefers to live their life on purpose should experience a Success

Road Map. For example, at BAI our Accountability Coaches facilitate the Success Road Map process for financial professionals (our specialty) and use their completed Success Road Map as the framework and basis to help them build a community of ideal clients and improve their quality of life.

Any leader, mentor, or coach can do the same for his or her people. And if you don't have a person like this in your life you can do it for yourself.

By the way, age is not a factor. If you have a future, then having a Success Road Map will help you make the most of it. You're never too old to plan your future. As Peter Drucker, the legendary management guru, once said, "The best way to predict your future is to create it."

Wright

How do you create a Success Road Map?

Bachrach

The best way is to have a leader, mentor, or a coach facilitate your journey through the process and capture your answers on the Success Road Map document. Or, as mentioned earlier, you can do it for yourself or with a friend by following the instructions in this chapter.

Before you begin to fill in your Success Road Map, read this chapter all the way through and then come back and complete each part of the Success Road Map.

There are three core elements of the Success Road Map. Let's consider them one at a time.

The Values Conversation™ (staircase in upper right-hand section)

The first element of the Success Road Map is the Values Conversation. Values are the "emotional why" behind the "tangible what" of your goals. Roy Disney, Walt's brother, is famous for having said, "When your values are clear your decisions are easy."

You wouldn't have invested in a book titled *Roadmap to Success* or considered building your *Success* Road Map if success weren't important to you. And "success" means different things to different people. So, the question that drives this part of the Success Road Map is, "What's *important* about 'success' to *you?*"

Step 1: Write the word "success" in the bottom step of the Values Staircase˜ as illustrated here.

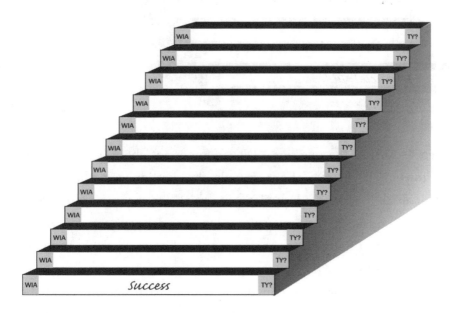

Step 2: Answer the question: "What's important about 'success' to you?"

Step 3: Write *your* answer in the blank step above where you wrote "success" on the Values Staircase. For example, as illustrated in the following staircase diagram, if your answer was "financial independence" you would write that on the step above "Success."

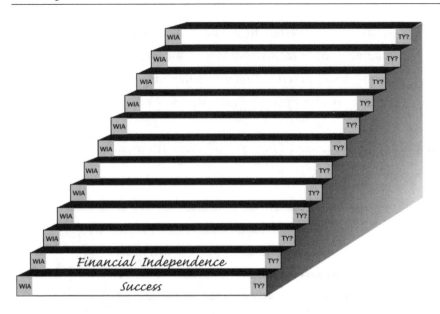

Step 4: Answer the question, "What's important about 'your previous answer' to you?" In the case of our example, the question would be, "What's important about 'financial independence' to you?" On the one hand, there's no time limit, so take all the time you need to consider your answer. On the other hand, the first thing that pops into your head is usually the best answer to write in the next step of the staircase.

Step 5: Write your answer in the next blank step, moving from the bottom to the top of the Values Staircase, as illustrated in the following diagram. In this case, the answer "security" is written in the next step moving up the staircase.

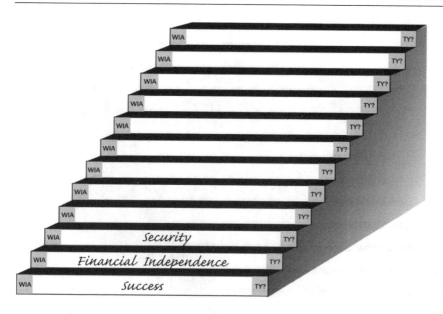

Continue to answer the question "What's important about 'your previous answer' to you?" until you absolutely, no matter how much you think about it, cannot come up with any more answers.

It doesn't matter how long it takes. The further you go up the Values Staircase the better. If you have more answers than there are steps, continue up into the margin. There is no right or wrong number of answers. You will almost certainly have upward of seven to ten.

When your Values Staircase is complete it will likely contain three levels of values.

Your first few answers are usually more about the immediate, fundamental things that drive you. The answers above them tend to be things that matter to you about others such as family, friends, community, and/or the world. Your answers toward the top of the Values Staircase will probably be about the higher, more esoteric, philosophical, and spiritual things that matter to you, similar to Maslow's "self actualization" concept.

The following completed staircase is just for illustration purposes. It's important that when you do the exercise you really think for yourself and answer what's important *to you*.

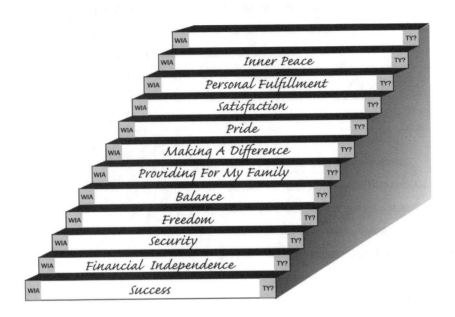

Goals Conversation™ (shields along bottom middle to right)

The second element of the Success Road Map is the Goals Conversation. For the purpose of your Success Road Map, your goals are the personal milestones that you use to measure your success in life. These are the big things like buying a home, financial independence, funding your children's or grandchildren's educations, establishing a foundation, building a successful business, etc. These goals tend to be things that require money and planning to achieve. (Items like your income, getting out of debt, your relationships, and health are covered in the third element of the Success Road Map.)

Each goal has 4 key elements:
1. Name
2. Target date: month/day/year
3. Amount of money wanted
4. Two to three words that describe what you will be thinking and feeling when you achieve the goal

Make sure your goals are really yours and not those that have been projected on to you by family, friends, or society. What do *you* really want to accomplish in your life?

Ask yourself the goal questions in order:

Step 1:

"What's a goal that requires money and planning to achieve?"

Write the name of the goal in the top line of one of the shields.

Step 2:

"By when do you want to achieve this goal?"

Be specific.

Write the month, day, and year in the next line of the goal shield.

Step 3:

"How much money do you need to achieve this goal?" For something like financial independence, ask yourself, "How much net, spendable money per month or per year do I need to be financially independent?" For goals like buying a home, break it down into down payment and home improvement money.

If you're not sure how much something costs, do your homework. Go online to research college tuition expenses, comps for real estate, or consult with advisors or experts in whatever areas you need help with. The more specific and accurate your goal the more compelling and motivating you will find it to be.

Step 4:

Make it more powerful by asking yourself, "What are two or three words that describe what I'm thinking and feeling once I have achieved this goal?"

Write these words in the bottom part of the shield.

The following illustrates what a completed goal looks like. Yours, of course, will be different because these are just examples.

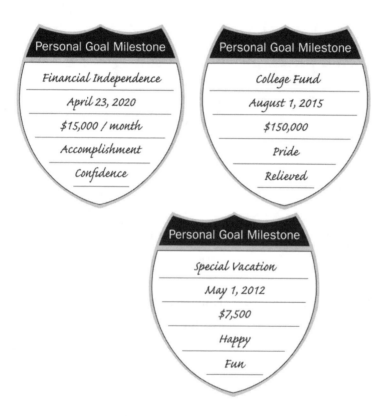

Your goals are the tangible *what* you want and your values are the emotional *why* you want it. The combination of the two increases the probability that you will actually do the work required to achieve your goals for the reasons that are important to you.

The Now/Be Conversation™ (lower left hand section)

The third element of the Success Road Map is the Now/Be Conversation. This conversation is driven by the question, "Where are you now and where do you want to be in key areas that relate to the achievement of your goals and your quality of life?"

This is another simple and fun exercise. List the categories that are relevant for you. Put a number that represents where you are now, where you want to be, and a date by when you want to be there.

The following are some possible categories to consider:

Gross revenue or production

Personal income

Debt

Net worth

Number of clients

Number of Ideal Clients

Revenue per client

Revenue per Ideal Client

Referrals

Business value

Work hours/day or week

Days or weeks of vacation per month or year

Fitness level

Weight

Body mass index

Calories consumed

Calories burned

Clothing size

Exercise or workouts/day or week

Stretching/day or week

Comprehensive physical exam

Blood work measures (e.g., cholesterol, triglycerides, etc., especially those that are of particular concern due to personal or family history)

Time with people you care about

Time with causes you care about

Prayer

Meditation

Fun

Most of these categories are easy to measure with money, standard measures for your particular business or career, a scale of one to ten, or a percentage scale.

Remember, this is just a partial list of possibilities and on the following diagram I just made up the numbers to illustrate what it could look like when it's completed. You should not be influenced one way or the other by these numbers. First of all, some of the categories are not relevant for you and even if they are, your numbers can be higher or lower. The most important factor is that you create something that is relevant and inspiring *for you*. You may also find that you build and modify elements of your Success Road Map over time.

Have fun creating your own!

CATEGORY	NOW	WANT TO BE	BY WHEN
Business Revenue	$250,000	$1M	12/31/2011
Personal income	$125,000	$500,000	4/15/2012
Debt	$25,000	0	1/1/2010
Net worth	$250,000	$2.5M	6/1/2020
# of clients	500	1,000	12/31/11
# of Ideal Clients	25	75	12/31/11
Revenue per client	$500	$1,000	12/31/11
Revenue per Ideal Client	$2,000	$7,500	12/31/11
Referrals	Not Many!	10 / month	11/09
Business value	$375,000	$1.5M	12/31/11
Work hours	50 / wk	35 / wk	12/31/11
Vacation	2 wks / year	6 wks/ year	1/1/10
Fitness level	5	8	9/27/09
Weight	175	160	9/27/09
Body Fat	20%	15%	9/27/09
Calories consumed	3,000 / day	2,200 / day	
Exercise	1 / wk	4 / wk	6/1/08
Stretching	0	2 / wk	6/1/08
Yoga	0	2 / wk	6/1/08
Comprehensive physical exam			5/15/08
HDL Cholesterol	30	50	5/5/10
Date nights	1 / wk	2 / wk	6/1/08
Hours w/ kids	10 / wk	15 / wk	6/1/08
TV news	7 hrs / wk	2 hrs / wk	7/4/08
$ to charity	5%	10%	1/1/10
Ski days	10 / yr	20 / yr	1/1/10

And this is what a completed Success Road Map looks like:

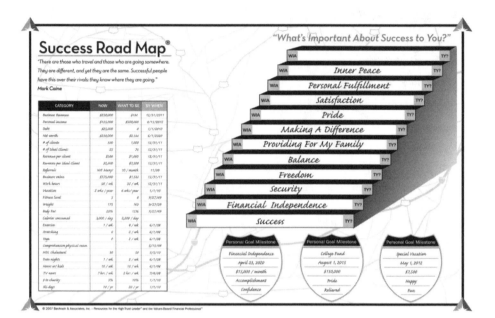

Wright

What do I do with my SRM once I have it?

Bachrach

Follow these guidelines:

- First of all, live with it for a week or so. Then review it again and make any appropriate changes.

- Discuss it with your spouse or a close friend. Ask for his or her opinion. Ask in a general way by saying something like, "I've built this tool for myself called the Success Road Map and I'm interested in your perspective on what I've written down here." Then just sit back and listen. Answer questions, but resist the temptation to over-explain or "sell" your Success Road Map. You don't have to change anything or do anything based on someone else's input. However, you might find the insights of others valuable for making better choices.

- Check the veracity of your "now/be" to your goals. Do some math. For example, there are times when our coaches recognize a disconnect between a financial advisor's goals and their "now/be." We've seen a goal of two hundred thousand dollars per year of net income in retirement, yet their financial net worth "be" target is only one million dollars. The problem is the need for a 20 percent ROI to maintain the desired retirement income at a time when riskier investments would not be prudent.

- Think. Create a plan. Take action.

- Write a business plan that supports your Success Road Map.

- Create a strategic plan that supports your Success Road Map.

- Develop tactics that support your Success Road Map.

- Build a Personal Inspiration Board™. This is simple to make and may remind you of a junior high school project where you made a collage. The adult version is an excellent tool to help you live a great life. Here's all you have to do: Buy a very large corkboard. Secure your Success Road Map in the center with staples or thumbtacks. Then surround your Success Road Map with pictures, sayings, quotes, and anything else inspiring that relates to the actualization of your Success Road Map. Hang it in a prominent place where you will see it so you stay on track to do the work your goals require to achieve them. Remember Peter Vidmar's comment about being a champion, "To be a champion you only have to do two things: work out when you feel like it, and work out when you *don't* feel like it." If you're a motivated prodigy who stays focused and on track 24–7 and 365 days a year, maybe you don't need a tool like the Personal Inspiration Board. The rest of us mortals can use all the help we can get.

- Use your Success Road Map to plan your calendar. The bottom line is that there are 168 hours in the week. How you use these 168 hours determines your success and quality of life. Does your planned calendar reflect your priorities, your goals, and your values? If so, fantastic! If not, fix it—now.

- Consider hiring a coach who can help you organize your calendar around your priorities and then actually hold you accountable to honor your calendar.

Wright

Bill, how can readers get a copy of the Success Road Map to complete for themselves?

Bachrach

Send an e-mail to SRMRequest@baivbfp.com to request your complimentary Success Road Map. If you are a financial advisor, you can call 800-347-3707 and schedule a complimentary consultation with one of our coaches to have your Success Road Map completed.

Wright

Is there anything else you think I should know about the Success Road Map?

Bachrach

In any endeavor, personal or professional, there are always a handful of activities that produce most of the results. Your Success Road Map will help you identify those key activities and help you stay focused on actually doing those key activities for longer periods of time.

When the inevitable crush of too much to do and not enough time takes you away from your priorities, your Success Road Map can help you reconnect to your priorities, get you back on track, and stay on track longer, thus producing better and more consistent results.

Do more than just read about the Success Road Map. Create your own Success Road Map and do the work to make it happen.

About the Author

Bill Bachrach, CSP, is Founder and Chairman of Bachrach & Associates, Inc. (BAI). BAI is a well-known training and development company for financial professionals. Established in 1988, BAI has a full complement of training, coaching, and support services to help financial professionals implement Values-Based Financial Planning™. In addition, Bill is a best-selling author and an accomplished keynote speaker. He and his wife, Anne, live in La Jolla, California, where they lead an active lifestyle.

Bill Bachrach, CSP
8380 Miramar Mall, Suite 200
San Diego, CA 92121
800.347.3707
www.baivbfp.com

ROADMAP to SUCCESS 3

An interview with...

Dr. Stephen Covey

David E. Wright (Wright)

We're talking today with Dr. Stephen R. Covey, cofounder and vice-chairman of Franklin Covey Company, the largest management company and leadership development organization in the world. Dr. Covey is perhaps best known as author of *The 7 Habits of Highly Effective People,* which is ranked as a number one best-seller by the *New York Times,* having sold more than fourteen million copies in thirty-eight languages throughout the world. Dr. Covey is an internationally respected leadership authority, family expert, teacher, and organizational consultant. He has made teaching principle-centered living and principle-centered leadership his life's work. Dr. Covey is the recipient of the Thomas More College Medallion for Continuing Service to Humanity and has been awarded four honorary doctorate degrees. Other awards given Dr. Covey include the Sikh's 1989 International Man of Peace award, the 1994 International Entrepreneur of the Year award, *Inc.* magazine's Services Entrepreneur of the Year award, and in 1996 the National Entrepreneur of the Year Lifetime Achievement award for Entrepreneurial leadership. He has also been recognized as one of *Time* magazine's twenty-five most influential Americans and one of *Sales and Marketing Management's* top twenty-five power brokers. As the father of nine and grandfather of forty-four, Dr. Covey received the 2003 National Fatherhood Award, which he says is the most meaningful award he has ever received. Dr. Covey earned his undergraduate degree from the University of Utah, his MBA from Harvard, and completed his doctorate at Brigham Young University. While at Brigham Young he served as assistant to the President and was also a professor of Business Management and Organizational Behavior.

Dr. Covey, welcome to *Roadmap to Success.*

Dr. Stephen Covey (Covey)

Thank you.

Wright

Dr. Covey, most companies make decisions and filter them down through their organization. You, however, state that no company can succeed until individuals within it succeed. Are the goals of the company the result of the combined goals of the individuals?

Covey

Absolutely—if people aren't on the same page, they're going to be pulling in different directions. To teach this concept, I frequently ask large audiences to close their eyes and point north, and then to keep pointing and open their eyes. They find themselves pointing all over the place. I say to them, "Tomorrow morning if you want a similar experience, ask the first ten people you meet in your organization what the purpose of your organization is and you'll find it's a very similar experience. They'll point all over the place." When people have a different sense of purpose and values, every decision that is made from then on is governed by those. There's no question that this is one of the fundamental causes of misalignment, low trust, interpersonal conflict, interdepartmental rivalry, people operating on personal agendas, and so forth.

Wright

Is that primarily a result of an inability to communicate from the top?

Covey

That's one aspect, but I think it's more fundamental. There's an inability to involve people—an unwillingness. Leaders may communicate what their mission and their strategy is, but that doesn't mean there's any emotional connection to it. Mission statements that are rushed and then announced are soon forgotten. They become nothing more than just a bunch of platitudes on the wall that mean essentially nothing and even create a source of cynicism and a sense of hypocrisy inside the culture of an organization.

Wright

How do companies ensure survival and prosperity in these tumultuous times of technological advances, mergers, downsizing, and change?

Covey

I think that it takes a lot of high trust in a culture that has something that doesn't change—principles—at its core. There are principles that people agree upon that are valued. It gives a sense of stability. Then you have the power to adapt and be flexible when you experience these kinds of disruptive new economic models or technologies that come in and sideswipe you. You don't know how to handle them unless you have something you can depend upon.

If people have not agreed to a common set of principles that guide them and a common purpose, then they get their security from the outside and they tend to freeze the structure, systems, and processes inside and they cease becoming adaptable. They don't change with the changing realities of the new marketplace out there and gradually they become obsolete.

Wright

I was interested in one portion of your book, *The 7 Habits of Highly Effective People,* where you talk about behaviors. How does an individual go about the process of replacing ineffective behaviors with effective ones?

Covey

I think that for most people it usually requires a crisis that humbles them to become aware of their ineffective behaviors. If there's not a crisis the tendency is to perpetuate those behaviors and not change.

You don't have to wait until the marketplace creates the crisis for you. Have everyone accountable on a 360-degree basis to everyone else they interact with—with feedback either formal or informal—where they are getting data as to what's happening. They will then start to realize that the consequences of their ineffective behavior require them to be humble enough to look at that behavior and to adopt new, more effective ways of doing things.

Sometimes people can be stirred up to this if you just appeal to their conscience—to their inward sense of what is right and wrong. A lot of people sometimes know inwardly they're doing wrong, but the culture doesn't necessarily discourage them from continuing that. They either need feedback from people or they need feedback from the marketplace or they need feedback from their conscience. Then they can begin to develop a step-by-step process of replacing old habits with new, better habits.

Wright

It's almost like saying, "Let's make all the mistakes in the laboratory before we put this thing in the air."

Covey

Right; and I also think what is necessary is a paradigm shift, which is analogous to having a correct map, say of a city or of a country. If people have an inaccurate paradigm of life, of other people, and of themselves it really doesn't make much difference what their behavior or habits or attitudes are. What they need is a correct paradigm—a correct map—that describes what's going on.

For instance, in the Middle Ages they used to heal people through bloodletting. It wasn't until Samuel Weiss and Pasteur and other empirical scientists discovered the germ theory that they realized for the first time they weren't dealing with the real issue. They realized why women preferred to use midwives who washed rather than doctors who didn't wash. They gradually got a new paradigm. Once you've got a new paradigm then your behavior and your attitude flow directly from it. If you have a bad paradigm or a bad map, let's say of a city, there's no way, no matter what your behavior or your habits or your attitudes are—how positive they are—you'll never be able to find the location you're looking for. This is why I believe that to change paradigms is far more fundamental than to work on attitude and behavior.

Wright

One of your seven habits of highly effective people is to "begin with the end in mind." If circumstances change and hardships or miscalculations occur, how does one view the end with clarity?

Covey

Many people think to begin with the end in mind means that you have some fixed definition of a goal that's accomplished and if changes come about you're not going to adapt to them. Instead, the "end in mind" you begin with is that you are going to create a flexible culture of high trust so that no matter what comes along you are going to do whatever it takes to accommodate that new change or that new reality and maintain a culture of high performance and high trust. You're talking more in terms of values and overall purposes that don't change, rather than specific strategies or programs that will have to change to accommodate the changing realities in the marketplace.

Wright

In this time of mistrust among people, corporations, and nations, for that matter, how do we create high levels of trust?

Covey

That's a great question and it's complicated because there are so many elements that go into the creating of a culture of trust. Obviously the most fundamental one is just to have trustworthy people. But that is not sufficient because what if the organization itself is misaligned?

For instance, what if you say you value cooperation but you really reward people for internal competition? Then you have a systemic or a structure problem that creates low trust inside the culture even though the people themselves are trustworthy. This is one of the insights of Edward Demming and the work he did. That's why he said that most problems are not personal—they're systemic. They're common caused. That's why you have to work on structure, systems, and processes to make sure that they institutionalize principle-centered values. Otherwise you could have good people with bad systems and you'll get bad results.

When it comes to developing interpersonal trust between people, it is made up of many, many elements such as taking the time to listen to other people, to understand them, and to see what is important to them. What we think is important to another may only be important to us, not to another. It takes empathy. You have to make and keep promises to them. You have to treat people with kindness and courtesy. You have to be completely honest and open. You have to live up to your commitments. You can't betray people behind their back. You can't badmouth them behind their back and sweet-talk them to their face. That will send out vibes of hypocrisy and it will be detected.

You have to learn to apologize when you make mistakes, to admit mistakes, and to also get feedback going in every direction as much as possible. It doesn't necessarily require formal forums—it requires trust between people who will be open with each other and give each other feedback.

Wright

My mother told me to do a lot of what you're saying now, but it seems that when I got in business I simply forgot.

Covey

Sometimes we forget, but sometimes culture doesn't nurture it. That's why I say unless you work with the institutionalizing—that means formalizing into structure, systems, and processing the values—you will not have a nurturing culture. You have to constantly work on that.

This is one of the big mistakes organizations make. They think trust is simply a function of being honest. That's only one small aspect. It's an important aspect, obviously, but there are so many other elements that go into the creation of a high-trust culture.

Wright

"Seek first to understand then to be understood" is another of your seven habits. Do you find that people try to communicate without really understanding what other people want?

Covey

Absolutely. The tendency is to project out of our own autobiography—our own life, our own value system—onto other people, thinking we know what they want. So we don't really listen to them. We pretend to listen, but we really don't listen from within their frame of reference. We listen from within our own frame of reference and we're really preparing our reply rather than seeking to understand. This is a very common thing. In fact, very few people have had any training in seriously listening. They're trained in how to read, write, and speak, but not to listen.

Reading, writing, speaking, and listening are the four modes of communication and they represent about two-thirds to three-fourths of our waking hours. About half of that time is spent listening, but it's the one skill people have not been trained in. People have had all this training in the other forms of communication. In a large audience of 1,000 people you wouldn't have more than twenty people who have had more than two weeks of training in listening. Listening is more than a skill or technique; you must listen within another's frame of reference. It takes tremendous courage to listen because you're at risk when you listen. You don't know what's going to happen; you're vulnerable.

Wright

Sales gurus always tell me that the number one skill in selling is listening.

Covey

Yes—listening from within the customer's frame of reference. That is so true. You can see that it takes some security to do that because you don't know what's going to happen.

Wright

With this book we're trying to encourage people to be better, to live better, and be more fulfilled by listening to the examples of our guest authors. Is there anything or anyone in your life that has made a difference for you and helped you to become a better person?

Covey

I think the most influential people in my life have been my parents. I think that what they modeled was not to make comparisons and harbor jealousy or to seek recognition. They were humble people.

I remember one time when my mother and I were going up in an elevator and the most prominent person in the state was also in the elevator. She knew him, but she spent her time talking to the elevator operator. I was just a little kid and I was so awed by the famous person. I said to her, "Why didn't you talk to the important person?" She said, "I was. I had never met him."

My parents were really humble, modest people who were focused on service and other people rather than on themselves. I think they were very inspiring models to me.

Wright

In almost every research paper I've ever read, those who write about people who have influenced their lives include three teachers in their top-five picks. My seventh-grade English teacher was the greatest teacher I ever had and she influenced me to no end.

Covey

Would it be correct to say that she saw in you probably some qualities of greatness you didn't even see in yourself?

Wright

Absolutely.

Covey

That's been my general experience—the key aspect of a mentor or a teacher is someone who sees in you potential that you don't even see in yourself. Those teachers/mentors treat you accordingly and eventually you come to see it in yourself. That's my definition of leadership or influence—

communicating people's worth and potential so clearly that they are inspired to see it in themselves.

Wright

Most of my teachers treated me as a student, but she treated me with much more respect than that. As a matter of fact, she called me Mr. Wright, and I was in the seventh grade at the time. I'd never been addressed by anything but a nickname. I stood a little taller; she just made a tremendous difference.

Do you think there are other characteristics that mentors seem to have in common?

Covey

I think they are first of all good examples in their own personal lives. Their personal lives and their family lives are not all messed up—they come from a base of good character. They also are usually very confident and they take the time to do what your teacher did to you—to treat you with uncommon respect and courtesy.

They also, I think, explicitly teach principles rather than practices so that rules don't take the place of human judgment. You gradually come to have faith in your own judgment in making decisions because of the affirmation of such a mentor. Good mentors care about you—you can feel the sincerity of their caring. It's like the expression, "I don't care how much you know until I know how much you care."

Wright

Most people are fascinated with the new television shows about being a survivor. What has been the greatest comeback that you've made from adversity in your career or your life?

Covey

When I was in grade school I experienced a disease in my legs. It caused me to use crutches for a while. I tried to get off them fast and get back. The disease wasn't corrected yet so I went back on crutches for another year. The disease went to the other leg and I went on for another year. It essentially took me out of my favorite thing—athletics—and it took me more into being a student. So that was a life-defining experience, which at the time seemed very negative, but has proven to be the basis on which I've focused my life—being more of a learner.

Wright

Principle-centered learning is basically what you do that's different from anybody I've read or listened to.

Covey

The concept is embodied in the Far Eastern expression, "Give a man a fish, you feed him for the day; teach him how to fish, you feed him for a lifetime." When you teach principles that are universal and timeless, they don't belong to just any one person's religion or to a particular culture or geography. They seem to be timeless and universal like the ones we've been talking about here: trustworthiness, honesty, caring, service, growth, and development. These are universal principles. If you focus on these things, then little by little people become independent of you and then they start to believe in themselves and their own judgment becomes better. You don't need as many rules. You don't need as much bureaucracy and as many controls and you can empower people.

The problem in most business operations today—and not just business but non-business—is that they're using the industrial model in an information age. Arnold Toynbee, the great historian, said, "You can pretty well summarize all of history in four words: nothing fails like success." The industrial model was based on the asset of the machine. The information model is based on the asset of the person—the knowledge worker. It's an altogether different model. But the machine model was the main asset of the twentieth century. It enabled productivity to increase fifty times. The new asset is intellectual and social capital—the qualities of people and the quality of the relationship they have with each other. Like Toynbee said, "Nothing fails like success." The industrial model does not work in an information age. It requires a focus on the new wealth, not capital and material things.

A good illustration that demonstrates how much we were into the industrial model, and still are, is to notice where people are on the balance sheet. They're not found there. Machines are found there. Machines become investments. People are on the profit-and-loss statement and people are expenses. Think of that—if that isn't bloodletting.

Wright

It sure is.

When you consider the choices you've made down through the years, has faith played an important role in your life?

Covey

It has played an extremely important role. I believe deeply that we should put principles at the center of our lives, but I believe that God is the source of those principles. I did not invent them. I get credit sometimes for some of the Seven Habits material and some of the other things I've done, but it's really all based on principles that have been given by God to all of His children from the beginning of time. You'll find that you can teach these same principles from the sacred texts and the wisdom literature of almost any tradition. I think the ultimate source of that is God and that is one thing you can absolutely depend upon—"in God we trust."

Wright

If you could have a platform and tell our audience something you feel would help them or encourage them, what would you say?

Covey

I think I would say to put God at the center of your life and then prioritize your family. No one on their deathbed ever wished they had spent more time at the office.

ABOUT THE AUTHOR

Stephen R. Covey was recognized in 1996 as one of *Time* magazine's twenty-five most influential Americans and one of *Sales and Marketing Management's* top twenty-five power brokers. Dr. Covey is the author of several acclaimed books, including the international bestseller, *The 7 Habits of Highly Effective People*, named the number one Most Influential Business Book of the Twentieth Century, and other best sellers that include *First Things First, Principle-Centered Leadership*, (with sales exceeding one million) and *The 7 Habits of Highly Effective Families*.

Dr. Covey's newest book, *The 8th Habit: From Effectiveness to Greatness*, which was released in November 2004, rose to the top of several bestseller lists, including *New York Times, Wall Street Journal, USA Today, Money, Business Week*, Amazon.com, and Barnes & Noble.

Dr. Covey earned his undergraduate degree from the University of Utah, his MBA from Harvard, and completed his doctorate at Brigham Young University. While at Brigham Young University, he served as assistant to the President and was also a professor of Business Management and Organizational Behavior. He received the National Fatherhood Award in 2003, which, as the father of nine and grandfather of forty-four, he says is the most meaningful award he has ever received.

Dr. Covey currently serves on the board of directors for the Points of Light Foundation. Based in Washington, D.C., the Foundation, through its partnership with the Volunteer Center National Network, engages and mobilizes millions of volunteers from all walks of life—businesses, nonprofits, faith-based organizations, low-income communities, families, youth, and older adults—to help solve serious social problems in thousands of communities.

Dr. Stephen R. Covey
www.stephencovey.com

ROADMAP *to* SUCCESS 4

An interview with...

Mark Little

Wright

Today we are speaking with Mark Little. In 2004, Mark weighed 313 pounds and, while being a highly successful business owner, he was overweight, out of balance and very unhappy. But something happened, after 25 years of struggling with his weight, he made up his mind to get lighter and fitter. He dropped 140 pounds, through better eating and increased physical activity, and now weighs his high school weight of 173 pounds. Out of gratitude to his mentors and those who helped him get lighter and fitter, he agreed to mentor twelve non-athletes, like himself, during the first half of 2007. All twelve experienced personal physical transformations losing 321 pounds in total. The Fitness Race was born and now helps people worldwide get as light and fit as they choose, by following the same simple method that Mark followed for himself.

So, what has been your roadmap to success?

Little

My wake-up call came when my doctor told me he was dying. After struggling with my weight for more than twenty-five years, I finally decided to take charge of my health and fitness so that I could live to watch my daughter grow up and hopefully, walk her down the aisle someday. You see, I was in terrible shape physically.

After building, by nearly every measure, a successful financial advisory business, in October 2004 I found myself more than one hundred forty pounds overweight. I had serious diabetes problems, including periodic blindness and a painful form of arthritis that had me frequently taking wheelchair assistance at the airport. My cholesterol was so high that my doctor couldn't get a correct reading on it.

That's when Dr. Robert Still, my internal medicine doctor, chose to pose the question to me during my annual physical, "You think you're exempt, don't you?" Unaccustomed to this form of frankness I just stared back at him and he continued, "Mark, you are a three-hundred-and-thirteen-pound diabetic experiencing serious symptoms. There's no male in your family medical history that we can find who has achieved age fifty-five without having either a heart attack or bypass surgery and you're forty-seven. You think you're exempt, don't you?"

Clear that he was on a mission with me and had much to say, I wisely chose to listen quietly. He continued, "Mark, how important is it to you to see your eight-year-old daughter grow up, because at this pace I wouldn't put my money on your living even ten more years. Your only salvation is to get lighter and fitter starting today."

Wright

What went through your head as your doctor outlined the need for you to find a new roadmap for your life?

Little

My thought was, "Why now?" Why did he choose this annual physical to confront me after all these years of struggling with my weight? He confided with me that he had cancer and might not make it. That night I updated my Success Road Map®. You see, back in 1999 I met Bill Bachrach and had implemented this simple, compelling, one-page tool he had created to utilize with every client who worked with my financial services firm and it had been a gift of clarity for them. I had seen the life transformations that this single piece of paper had had on countless of my clients and now it was about to transform mine.

I proceeded to update and then implement my Success Road Map, which then inspired a simple plan that, after twenty-five years of struggling with my weight, ultimately saw me shed one hundred and forty pounds of excess weight. Dr. Still never lived to see the positive impact of his accountability session with me, but today I'm off all medications, my cholesterol is normal, my diabetes cannot be seen by any measurement, and I am now competing in three to four triathlons every year.

I could have simply enjoyed my newly found health, but it was on my heart to help others struggling with their weight. I felt that I had unlocked a revolutionary new secret to getting lighter and fitter and wondered if my method and process could be replicated by others. So, I gathered twelve friends who had struggled with their weight for years, as I had.

Wright

So you have used a roadmap to success process to inspire you, you updated your roadmap, and then decided to help others. What did you do after that?

Little

Well, let me jump ahead to August 26, 2007—I wish you could have been there as I celebrated with these twelve people the personal physical transformation they had seen in their lives that had started with the completion of their own Success Road Maps. I will never forget how I felt as I watched most of them cross the finish line of the Chicago Accenture Triathlon, with almost nine thousand other athletes. A triathlon is a challenging event combining a swim, a bicycle race, and a run into a single race. A few chose other considerable and hefty physical goals, such as a one-hundred-kilometer bike race. This was one of the finest, most-prized moments of my life.

You see, just seven months earlier this group of non-athletes could not run a block or swim a lap in the pool and here they were now, swimming, bicycling, and running in the world's largest triathlon. Together the group lost three hundred and twenty-one pounds during the seven months they trained together for these events that literally had scared them to death just a few months earlier.

Wright

Wow! So you mentored twelve people to make major improvements with their physical health. You used the same roadmap to success that you utilized to inspire yourself. What an accomplishment for them. I'll bet they are grateful to you.

Little

Yes, they are grateful and we have founded TheFitnessRace.com as a result. The purpose of The Fitness Race™ is to provide people with the skill and confidence to get as light and fit as they want. The goal of The Fitness Race is to inspire and lead people to lose one billion pounds of excess weight and donate one dollar for every pound kept off, beginning with the first pound lost, to their favorite charity.

Wright

So having a clearly defined roadmap to success has helped The Fitness Race group think beyond themselves to larger issues such as charitable giving. What exactly is this roadmap tool that you use?

Little

Well, with The Fitness Race, just as with my affluent financial advisory clients, I started each participant off in the process with a Roadmap exercise which, on a single sheet of paper, gives participants a positive vision of their ideal future by helping them make the mental connection between their goals and those things that matter most to them in life, which are their deeply held values. The Success Roadmap is a simple but compelling exercise that clearly points out how to get from where you are now to where you want to be in order to experience the things that matter most to you.

I can walk you step-by-step through the Success Road Map process in a minute, but this Success Road Map forms the basis for establishing the necessary resolve to do "whatever it takes" and to persevere through inevitable discouragements that happen with any large goal in life.

Wright

So, the tool you use is an actual, physical road map that one fills out. That's great! So, what's the result of having this road map filled out?

Little

Having a roadmap and participating in The Fitness Race is all about creating a sensible plan and a path for getting you from where you are now to where you want to be with your weight, your fitness, and your health, utilizing the Success Roadmap as inspiration. I remember that Tom DeMarco, a well-known author and software engineer, is credited with this insightful nugget of wisdom, "You can't control what you can't measure." In the spirit of that quote as a launching pad for the great personal, professional, and physical transformation that is possible for anyone, we start with the Success Road Map, which is a clear summary of three things on one inspiring piece of paper. In this exercise you will clarify your values, establish goals that inspire you, and then benchmark your current situation with numbers that will allow you to measure success and progress benchmarked against the goals you have set for yourself.

You then update your benchmark measurements as you make progress and this Roadmap to Success becomes your dashboard for personal transformation and serves as your regularly updated progress report.

Wright

Okay, I get it—on this piece of paper you have those you mentor clarify their values and their goals. So Mark, what is the difference between a value and a goal? How do you describe the distinction between the two?

Little

Values are those deeply held beliefs that serve to guide and motivate you consciously and subconsciously. Values are the "why" behind the goals. They represent the hard wiring of your nature.

Let me share my values as an example for you. Values are simply those principles and ideals that are most important to you. So what's important about, say, "success" to me? Well, success is important because it allows me to pay my obligations, which gives me a sense of security and peace of mind. What's important about peace of mind to me is that it allows me to relax and focus on making a difference in the world by helping people to stretch and grow, which gives me a sense of achievement and joy. What's important about having that sense of joy to me is that I feel like I'm on the right track doing what I was put on earth to do and fulfilling the purpose God intended for me. Someday I want to have God look me in the eye and say "Well done good and faithful servant," which will give me a sense of fulfillment and ultimate peace.

Wright

So, a person's values are on a spectrum leading to things that are genuinely important to them—things that are important on a deep level, then?

Little

Right. You see, values exist on several levels with what you feel as your highest purpose being your highest values. The powerful thing about values is they provide that important compass in your life that gives you guidance.

People live their values whenever their actions are in close alignment with these things that matter most to them. For a complete guide of how to conduct an effective values conversation, or to have someone help you complete your entire Success Roadmap, go to http://thefitnessrace.com/roadmap.

Wright

Okay, so values are what drive people internally and motivate them to action. So how do you define a goal by comparison?

Little

Now that you have clarified your values and written them on your Success Roadmap, we can establish your goals. An effective goal has a name, a method of measurement, and a target date with a month, day, and year. For example, the name of the goal of The Fitness Race is "A billion pounds and a billion dollars." The specific goal is to lead people worldwide to lose at least one billion pounds of excess weight and to commit to donating or raising one dollar per year to their favorite charity for every pound they keep off by March 30, 2013. So in that goal, you see a method of measurement (one billion pounds lost, and one billion dollars per year going to charity) and a specific date that a participant can circle on his or her calendar.

Wright

So goals are milestones that we accomplish along the way in life?

Little

Exactly, and you can also easily see in this example how this goal lines up very well with my values—wanting to make a difference and help people stretch and grow, which gives me a sense that I'm fulfilling what I was put on earth to do.

Wright

How important are goals? Let's say an individual has deeply held values without having any goals. Isn't it good enough to just have dreams or aspirations and measure progress toward those?

Little

Yes, that is more than "good enough." However, if you have a goal that requires you to "get intentional" about your dreams, aspirations, and values, then the human mind does an almost magical thing. By converting your positive vision of your ideal future into specific goals, your dreams become tangible and measurable. By measuring progress, your dreams come alive and your daily behavior is affected. Think of a goal on your Success Roadmap as a focusing exercise allowing you to direct your valuable time—your most important resource—on activities that will drive the results of your goals.

It's hard to describe the excitement, momentum, and sense of urgency that is created when you have set a large meaningful goal and have the date circled on your calendar for this thing that currently scares you because you are not yet certain how you are going to pull it off. That's when the magic begins. The day before you set a specific target date for your goal, it's a pipe dream. Once you set that date, your goal becomes real. It begins to occur to you that you have to immediately get moving and get your calendar cleared sufficiently to make the effort necessary. Something clicks inside as you realize that the date you've committed to is now moving steadily toward you and will arrive whether you have made the necessary effort or not. The date doesn't care if you accomplish the goal or not. So you realize you'd better get intentional about it by planning, implementing, and preparing for the inevitable course-corrections ahead.

Wright

So, then, goals are important. Mark, once an individual you are advising sets a goal, what's the next step?

Little

Well, after setting your specific goal, taking this next mental step will help seal your resolve. As a final step in setting your goal it's helpful to take some advice from Bill Bachrach. In contemplating the achievement of your goal, write down a couple of words that will give a sense of how you will think or how you will feel once the goal's accomplished. This is just another beautiful way to check your resolve and create an inspirational thought that will sustain you when you really need it in the future. These words will give you yet another gut-check to ensure that the payoff is worth the effort you are about to make.

Wright

I know that words are important and powerful, but how have you seen these few words help people actualize their roadmap to success?

Little

Words are important and you should continually ponder this reality: we frequently know what we're supposed to do in order to accomplish our goals; the real question is "are we willing to cooperate by taking that first step?" One way to help increase the probability you will take action is to write down your goal and distribute it widely. Sharing your goal with as many other people as possible is part of the accountability that is so important to your success.

Wright

Yes, we have all had that experience of knowing the right things to do, but not being able to motivate ourselves to take action.

Little

Right, so after you have clarified your values and established specific goals, you are ready for the final step in creating your Success Road-Map—a very methodical benchmarking of your current situation. In order to establish a plan and a path to get you from where you are now to where you want to be by your target date, you need to know where you are now. That is called benchmarking.

There are many things you could measure as a means of benchmarking progress in the future toward your goals. The key is to measure those things that drive the result you want. For example, with my goal to get lighter and fitter, I benchmarked many things to measure progress, such as my weight, my body mass index, my body fat percentage, as well as my pants size, and other measures that would help me enjoy the process. But, I also benchmarked the three key activities that would ultimately drive the result I wanted:

1. The number of calories I ate per day
2. My hours spent doing physical training per week
3. My average heart rate for every hour of physical training

In my case, my team of experts set targets for these three key benchmarks. Your targets would be different, but mine were to eat 1,600 calories per day or less and train a minimum of four hours per week at an average heart rate of one hundred and thirty-five. With those three simple measures benchmarked and targeted for the future, I eventually lost and, more importantly, successfully kept off one hundred and forty pounds of excess weight.

If, for example, your goal were "more free time" then you would benchmark and measure how many days you are "taking off" now and then set a target going forward. If your goal is to make or invest a certain amount of money, then benchmark your current numbers and focus on how you will achieve your target.

By continually asking yourself how you are going to get from where your current benchmark is to your goal, you will begin envisioning creative and new paths to your goals.

Wright

Mark, you mentioned earlier that having a roadmap is all about creating a plan. Do you recommend people take this roadmap and then develop a plan? What did you do in your journey to lose weight?

Little

Every instinct told me that, as with my business, this long journey to get lighter and fitter would start with mapping out a strategy inspired by my Success Road Map and then I would need to create a written step-by-step plan to begin taking action. Jim Rohn is an American business philosopher whose writings and lectures over the years have had a profound impact on me in my many business successes. I recall a saying that goes, "An apple a day keeps the doctor away." Jim said, "What if it's true?" His point was that every long journey starts with a first step and what if the first step to good health is an action as simple as eating an apple?

Results are all about taking action, and actions are generated by creating a plan around the question "How?" This could include questions such as, "How am I going to lose one hundred and forty pounds?" That question generates action steps. So, are you willing to take an action as small as eating an apple? If not, you're reading the wrong book.

Even with a Success Road Map in place as your focal point for inspiration, you are still responsible for following your written plan, measuring progress, maintaining your resolve, and eliminating excuses. Even after I had that conversation with Dr. Still and resolved to do whatever it took to get as light and fit as I was back in high school, I still had to deal with excuses. It's a reality of human nature that we make way too many excuses. Even after I made up my mind to lose all that weight, my big excuse involved one of the businesses I owned. I whined and complained about what a drain that business was on me, how much time and energy it was sapping from me, and how much of an obstacle it represented between me and my goal of being lean and fit.

Wright

Agreed Mark, we all make too many excuses in life, particularly when it comes to things as important as our health, but aren't they just a fact of life? I mean, what is someone to do when an important area of life is filled with so many excuses that it is discouraging?

Little

The most important thing you can do is focus on the things you can control. That's usually enough. By getting inspired by my Success Road Map to achieve my health and fitness goal, I decided that any obstacle to this goal was no longer acceptable in my life, so I sold that business. It took nearly two years to discern this next piece of the puzzle, but I eventually came to the realization that my complaints about that business were simply more excuses. I didn't need to sell that business to create four hours of increased physical activity per week or to slow down my out-of-control eating habits. The second piece of good news, however, was that now I knew this about myself. It became a turning point in my realization that we all have to recognize and declare war upon all the excuses we continually make.

So, when excuses mount I recommend that you examine your current reality. Do you ever find yourself saying, "Something is preventing me from accomplishing my goal"? If so, write down the excuse that is preventing you from taking personal responsibility for your condition, light a candle, and burn up the paper. Now that excuse is gone forever.

Wright

Wow, so you sold your business because you had decided it was just another excuse. How then did you finally get yourself on track and tackle your fitness and health goal?

Little

With my final excuse neatly out of the way, what dawned on me was a renewed sense urgency and a feeling that life is fleeting. This revelation kept me going, even when I was discouraged. I realized that the next twelve months would pass whether or not I was working on improving my health.

It also came to me that I may not know whether it is possible to accomplish my entire goal of losing one hundred and forty pounds within the next twelve months, but wouldn't it be sad if the next twelve months went by and I had not even tried? It was at least conceivable for me that if I put my mind to it, twelve months from now I could be a completely transformed person with a completely different body, fitness profile, and health outlook. I could literally move from being that guy who "could drop dead on the sidewalk at any moment" to someone who can look forward to a long, healthy, active, and fulfilling life. I might even live long enough to walk my little daughter down the aisle at her wedding.

The vision Dr. Still gave me had created a resolve in my mind that being unhealthy was no longer acceptable. I was ready to take on the challenge and I knew that with this decision made the going would not be easy, but with a Success Road Map complete, a written plan in front of me, and the resolve to implement my step-by-step plan, it was downhill from there, with only a couple more steps to go.

Wright

There are, indeed, a few steps to this, and the sequence seems important. You mentioned discouragement. If someone gives up on a goal, I'll speculate that getting discouraged or depressed or both is a big reason why. This has got to be a huge issue. What do you recommend people do if they get discouraged?

Little

One of the best pieces of advice I can give you as you contemplate this is to create a written "Plan for Discouragement." The first step in this process is to turn inward and begin an appreciation journal. I have come to the realization and belief that depression and discouragement cannot exist in the presence of gratitude. So if you will take a few minutes every day and journal (or blog) all the things you are grateful for, then you will have begun a wonderful plan to eliminate many of the things that might discourage you in the future. If you do this while gazing at your Roadmap to Success, then you'll create a "multiplier effect" for your Appreciation Journal and it will be an even more effective tool for you.

Wright

What a great idea—an actual plan for those times when you might get discouraged. When I get discouraged, sometimes the smallest, even unintentional, kind words from others make a big difference. Do you recommend people seek out others to encourage them?

Little

Yes. In my case can you imagine how different it was for me to go from a sedentary life to a physically active one? So, the question is how does someone like me get from zero physical training and no self-control over what I was eating to having the passionate desire to create a comprehensive written lifetime plan for my health and fitness to which I was committed and excited to implement? Well, believe it or not it happened, and it can happen for anyone. In a flash you can go from an unmotivated, out-of-balanced, overweight failure at diet and exercise (as I was) to an "inspiration in the making" for the millions who are struggling with their weight or any other goal.

Here was a key for me: I decided to recruit an Encouragement Team (ET) to give me positive affirmations and to hold me accountable to the commitments I made to myself. The highest purpose of the Success Road Map is that it gives you clarity and focus, but there are marvelous spillover benefits to having your Road Map completed. One chief side benefit of your Road Map is that it serves as a method of communicating clearly, in writing, with your ET about what you're trying to accomplish. On one page of paper it clearly and quickly tells your story and allows your Trusted Advisors to explore how they might help you. I set the primary objective of my ET to ensure that I continually had an updated written Plan for Discouragement in place that we would review often.

I enlisted a core group of people who cared about me, including Anne Bachrach. I hired her to be my Accountability Coach and Chief Encouragement Officer (CEO). I also hired a Registered Dietician and a physical trainer to very methodically benchmark my current situation, create a training and nutrition plan, and to help me implement it.

Wright

So you clearly value coaching and advice; have you ever wondered if you could have done it on your own?

Little

I could have attempted this big goal on my own, without seeking the knowledge, encouragement, and accountability of others, but it occurred to me that my do-it-yourself plan had not been working well for me. It reminds me of the old Frank Sinatra classic, "I Did It My Way." It's about a guy who has made bad choices rationalizing his life screw-ups. Many of us love to look back on things and think, like the song, "at least I did it my way." The only problem with that logic is that "Doing it My Way" is what got me into this mess. If I were capable of my own rescue, then I'd be a slim and fit guy. The ironic thing about the song "My Way" is that, in looking at the lyrics of the song, the Chairman of the Board is singing a warning by lamenting about all the things that went wrong in his life, but "at least I did it my way."

So, if I'm realistically not capable of my own rescue, then the most important affirmation to say to myself is "I'm determined to at least cooperate in my own rescue" by being coachable by my ET. By continually telling my ET what I needed from them (which was advice, guidance, positive affirmations, and accountability), I told myself over and over that my job in this process was the simplest—just do what I'm told. I immediately recognized this as my prime objective. But the key to surrounding yourself with Trusted Advisors lies in this next sentence. Surrounding yourself with Trusted Advisors is simply for the purpose of supporting what you frequently know you need to do and may have known what needed to have been done for a long time, but left to your own devices it wasn't happening.

Wright

So that's it then—you still own it and you decided that even if you have an ET on your side they simply support the accountability that you are holding yourself to internally.

Little

Exactly. To paraphrase Bill Bachrach again, the success you achieve can be directly linked to the quality of the plan under which you operate. Can you imagine if you took off on a trip from Florida to California and rather than take a map, your friends just pointed and told you to head "that way," which took you through Virginia and New York? Wouldn't it make more sense to have a map with you—a map like your Success Road Map? Yet, it's amazing how many distractions and urgent disturbances from others we're willing to accept. Your ET will help you keep your focus on your Success Roadmap.

Wright

You mentioned that you advise people to focus on what they can control and you think most people have enough things within their control to accomplish their goals. Do you ever find that people are stuck in the past and have a hard time letting negative things go?

Little

One of the things that distinguishes the Success Road Map from simple goal setting is the focus of the exercise. By getting very clear about your values first, then establishing goals, and finally benchmarking where you are now, your Success Road Map focuses on the future in a very unique way. It allows you to recognize that your goals are simply a means to an end. The achievement of your goals is simply the evidence that you have made smart choices with your time and resources so you can experience your values. Like a coach, your ET encourages you to focus on your Success Road Map. A good coach on your ET will consistently say things like "Okay, here's what the next step is" or "How would be the best way to address that?" The desire of a great coach is to understand the past only to "benchmark" the current reality in order to measure progress in the future. Coaches like those on your ET serve to inspire you with your Success Road Map as a tool rather than waste of time and energy directing your focus on any past failures or shortcomings.

Positive results typically come from positive activity and avoidance of unwanted behavior. So, for the purposes of what you're doing to accomplish the goals on your Success Road Map, all in the past is now forgiven; focus on the future. Forgive yourself and others for all past failures! Forget and simply allow your Success Roadmap to make you focus on the future. Your ET can help you do that.

Wright

So with the Success Road Map complete, a written plan in place, and your Encouragement Team on board you began taking action. How did you measure progress?

Little

Well, my initial goal was to drop from three hundred and thirteen pounds down one hundred and ninety-five pounds by November 2, 2005, beginning on Tuesday November 2, 2004. Therefore, my goal was one hundred and eighteen pounds to be lost in one year's time, which I would actually accomplish in eight months and eight days. Ultimately, I would pick up triathlons as a sport to keep the weight off. Once I set doing triathlons as my next goal, my weight dropped from one hundred ninety-five to one hundred and seventy-three, which is what I weighed in high school (when I spent much time swimming, bicycling, and running around with no need to set a triathlon goal).

The Success Road Map is a wonderful progress report. Now that you have the three critical elements on one sheet of paper—your values, your goals, and your current situation benchmarked—it is easy to measure progress. First, let's define how we are going to measure progress. As simple as it sounds, for our purposes, we measure progress against the goal. So at least every three to four months you will update the benchmark section of your Success Road Map.

If your goal was to have more free time by taking twenty "travel days" before December 31 of this year, then every three to four months measure how many days you have taken actually taken off to see if you're on track to achieving that goal. By updating that benchmark measurement called "Number of 'Days Off' Traveling" you will easily be able to measure progress.

Wright

Is it possible to measure progress too frequently? I know that it could get discouraging, say, to jump on the scales every day and one day see no weight lost or even worse, an increase in weight.

Little

Yes, but the main idea is not to get distracted with noise or even worse, to measure things that are less relevant. I see this all the time when I consult with high-end financial advisors. Many of them feel that they need to update and educate their clients on the increase or decrease in the financial markets as a way of measuring progress. I patiently counsel them that clients could care less about what the markets are doing, but care deeply about their progress toward their goals. For example, if a client has a goal to purchase a lake home where the entire family can gather to have fun, then they don't care how much the market has moved up or down. What they want to know are two things: first, "how much money will I need before I can afford to buy that lake home?" (the goal), and second, "how much do I currently have that is earmarked for that goal?"

Wright

Sounds like simple measurements are best, especially the key ones that drive the result of the goal you're trying to achieve.

Little

That's it! In that example, a simple dollar-to-dollar measure of progress telling them how much they need versus how much they have now and whether that updated number is on track to their target date or not is what they want. If they are on track, that is great. If not, then a course correction may be necessary, but either way, the progress report is simple and doesn't involve any conversation or analysis of things that cannot be controlled, like the financial markets. There may be a recommendation to reallocate or redeploy assets differently that is within our control; but any energy spent on predicting those things outside of our control is silly.

On my journey to lose one hundred and forty pounds, I had unfailing belief that if my daily calories were under sixteen hundred, my weekly training hours were over four, and my average heart rate was over one hundred and thirty-five for those training hours—all things within my control—then the key benchmark on my Success Road Map (my weight) would come down, which it did.

Since I recommend updating the "benchmarking" section of the Success Road Map as your key progress report, be certain to keep all your past Success Road Maps so you can easily see the progress you have made.

Wright

I can imagine that many of the goals you see on peoples' Road Map require a lot of effort. It takes time to accomplish big things in life; everybody is busy these days. Do you ever run across people who say they just don't have the time?

Little

The most important resource we have is time. Bill Bachrach has coined the term "The Rule of 168." There are one hundred and sixty-eight hours in each week. It doesn't matter whether you are a cab driver, an office worker, or the head of a nation, we all get one hundred and sixty-eight hours each week. Our quality of life is determined by how we invest those hours. We can choose to spend our time doing many good things with those hours. Some choose to read financial magazines or watch television or discuss the news with those around us. I would never argue that those aren't good uses of your time. They may well be. But the real question is whether they are the *best use* of your time?

If you contemplate those things that matter most to you on your Success Road Map that are your highest, most prized values, you will notice something interesting. They are most likely related to things that are more important to you than money. They might include things like health and physical fitness, relationship fitness, career fitness, spiritual fitness, and things that point you toward the purpose of your life. So, contemplate your Success Road Map with just three simple, compelling pieces of information on it: where you are now (your benchmark), where you want to be (your goals), for the reasons that are important to you (your values). As you reflect on your values, are you spending your one hundred and sixty-eight hours each week on the best things? Are you respecting The Rule of 168 by planning your calendar around those things that will drive your goals so you can experience your values?

Wright

So then, what is the purpose of The Fitness Race movement you have launched?

Little

The purpose of The Fitness Race community of participants worldwide is to provide training and nutrition advice to participants so that they are inspired to make health a priority, which successful participants have learned brings life into better balance. Many participants have seen this improved balance lead to more confidence in all areas, empowering them to encourage and inspire each other while having fun doing it. Each participant agrees to "Take on" another participant and to hold that person accountable, which creates a great sense of fellowship and community. The goal of each participant is to be healthy and active, and to lead by example, allowing them the authority and desire to pay it forward to others who are struggling with their weight.

The vision of The Fitness Race is to inspire participants toward a lifestyle change to better health and fitness so they can be as light and as fit as they choose for life, empowering them to opt for optimal health and longevity and, in the end, make God-honoring decisions about their bodies. The goal of The Fitness Race is to inspire and lead people to lose one billion pounds of excess weight and donate one billion dollars annually to charity before March 30, 2013.

Wright

Well that's a big goal. This has been great, Mark. If you could recommend just one thing for people to do next to help put them on the road to success, what would it be?

Little

This entire chapter has led to my single simple call to action. As a result of reading this, I'm going to recommend one straightforward action step for you and see if you'll take it. After all this buildup, are you ready for my best recommendation and call for you to act? What I feel will serve you the most at this point is to come to our Web site at www.TheFitnessRace.com and join The Fitness Race. There's no cost, and it is the same place everyone who has seen big results with The Fitness Race began. That's it! That's what I recommend for people at this point.

By entering your name and e-mail address you will have made that most important first step to take charge of your health and fitness. You will love what happens next. Rather than being bombarded with e-mails "hammering" you to watch what you eat and go to the gym, instead you will receive a free four-page copy of my success story to inspire you and share with others you care about who are struggling with their weight. You will also receive a five-day mini-electronic course on specifically what to do next (whether or not you want to participate in a physical event or athletic race). This electronic course will give you practical tips and useful step-by-step guidance about what to do to immediately begin making progress (even if you never intend to participate fully in The Fitness Race). Finally, by entering your name and e-mail address to sign up for The Fitness Race, you will receive constructive and optimistic e-mails periodically from "Your Conscience" designed to be highly positive and encouraging affirmations and advice about how you can do what I did and choose to get as light and fit as you want.

I established The Fitness Race because of my daughter with the hope that she, and every reader of this chapter, will choose optimal health and longevity as a high priority goal in your life. By joining us in The Fitness Race you will become part of a revolution in health and fitness being launched that is allowing people to experience things that matter most to them in life.

I tell everyone I meet who struggles with their weight that I wish them future success because I have faith in them. I have hope that they will recognize the beautiful potential that they have to create an amazing personal transformation for themselves, regardless of past failures, and the inspiration they will be to others for what they have done.

And, finally, it is in the spirit of charity that I anticipate all the funding and support you will provide to a non-profit that you love by agreeing to donate one dollar per year for every pound you keep off, beginning with the first pound you lose. Regardless of what anyone does next, I want people to know this: when you're ready, we'll be here with arms wide open, encouraging and supporting your decision to join us.

Wright

Today we've been talking with Mark McKenna Little. Something happened to him after twenty-five years of struggling with his weight—he made up his mind to get lighter and fitter and he dropped one hundred and forty pounds. Today he's been talking about some of the things that we can do to do what he did and follow in his fitness race. I don't know about you but I'm going to visit the www.TheFitnessRace.com site as soon as I hang up the telephone. I'm going to sign up and maybe I can be a part of The Fitness Race.

Mark, thank you so much for being with us in *Roadmap to Success.*

About the Author

Mark McKenna Little is the founder, creator and author of The Fitness Race; How I lost 140 pounds... and you can lose as much as you want! After struggling with his weight for over 25 years he created a step-by-step process to lose all of his excess weight forever. He now mentors people all over the world through TheFitnessRace.com to get as light and fit as they want.

Professionally, Mark is the founder and creator of The Freedom Experience® Financial advisory firm for the highly affluent, which, for more than 20 years, has provided life coaching that specializes in money. The Freedom Experience® is a program focusing on helping the affluent take charge of their financial planning process by gaining clarity about what's most important to you first.

Originally from Houston, Texas Mark obtained his degree from Texas Christian University before embarking on a career in Finance. Mark started his own firm in 1987. His eleven year old daughter McKenna is the light of his life.

Mark McKenna Little
7660 Fay Avenue, H-111
La Jolla, CA 92037
888-467-8593
rapidresponse@TheFitnessRace.com
www.TheFitnessRace.com

An interview with...

Anne Bachrach

David Wright (Wright)

Today we're talking with Anne Bachrach. Anne is President of the California-based coaching firm A.M. Enterprises. For nearly a quarter of a century she has worked to help businesspeople and entrepreneurs improve their productivity, profitability, and quality of life. Her coaching services are in high demand and she only works with clients who are truly serious about achieving all of their goals and living their dreams. The core attribute of Anne's methodology is accountability, hence her nickname, "The Accountability Pit Bull."

Through proven systems she inspires her clients to stay focused and take action on the highest payoff activity that leads to their ultimate professional and personal success. By utilizing her powerful processes, Anne's clients learn how to maximize their true potential and bring balance to their lives. She is here today to help us focus on proven systems that will constantly create that compelling motivation that inspires us to take the most important action necessary to accomplish our largest goals so that we can ultimately enjoy what is truly important to us in our lives.

Anne, welcome to *Roadmap to Success.*

Anne Bachrach (Bachrach)

Thank you, David.

Wright

So, what is an accountability coach?

Bachrach

The number one reason that stops people from achieving what they truly want is lack of accountability. From my perspective, an accountability coach is a person whose sole objective is to help you achieve the goals that are truly important to you so you can experience a great quality of life. My job is to help people stay focused on their highest pay-off activities so they can achieve their goals in the timeframe that they set.

Accountability coaching uses proven systems and methods, like a road map for success, to inspire confidence and results in clients. Clients will develop an enhanced sense of self-esteem and accomplishment, which will allow them to realize that their biggest goals and dreams are within reach. In fact, clients often realize that their aspirations are not only doable, but they will also gain the energy necessary to create the incredible positive momentum required for achieving their goals.

My clients consider me the person in their life who helps them accelerate their results. There are too many distractions in life that prevent most people from focusing on the "right" activities to achieve all their goals. We get caught up in the day-to-day aspects of life and lose sight of the forward momentum necessary to take us to the next level. An accountability coach is someone who will take an honest look at you and your life and provide fresh insight. An accountability coach will help you enhance your quality of life. As a great symphony is brought to beautiful music by a conductor, an accountability coach orchestrates the instruments of your life to bring harmony.

Wright

Couldn't a trusted friend or colleague provide the same type of guidance?

Bachrach

I don't believe that a friend or colleague can provide the same level of guidance a coach can provide. After all, most people have their own agenda. Sometimes the other people in your life hold you back or hold you down, often quite unintentionally. Your spouse, your best friend, or your employees are not likely to point out the hard truths necessary for your personal growth.

The reality is, your friends or family do not want to hear the "hard truths" from you. Even when we are aware of our faults, we like to believe that these flaws are hidden or invisible from the rest of the world. A loved one, peer, colleague, or employee telling you hard truths about your life is not often going to give you the best results, no matter how good his or her intentions might be.

That's where an accountability coach steps in. You hire the coach because you want to make better, faster progress and see tangible results in your life. You're willing to let an accountability coach point out the tough stuff because this person is not your friend. You hired him or her exclusively for the purpose of helping you grow and achieve your goals.

Wright

So what does an accountability coach do?

Bachrach

The title says it all. An accountability coach holds you accountable for your goals and your life vision, pointing out the steps necessary to achieve your objectives. An accountability coach cares about helping you achieve the goals you set within the timeframes you desire. This type of coach helps you think outside the box and comes up with new strategies to assist you in moving from where you are now to where you want to be. What got you to where you are now may not be effective in getting you to where you want to be. You might have to get creative to move to your next level—and we all have a next level.

I want to clarify one thing. An accountability coach is not a therapist, a nutrition expert, or a fitness trainer. An accountability coach doesn't focus in on any one specific area of your life. The coach helps you improve all areas of your life to make you a better, more successful and well-rounded person. I will not work with a client exclusively on their professional life. The client has to set goals for all areas, including their relationships, physical environment, career, fitness, and health.

Your accountability coach is a "process expert"—someone guiding your journey and coaching you to your destination, with the end results accomplished by you. The coach allows you to invest in yourself. When appropriate, a coach will recommend other professionals or specialists who can assist you in achieving specific goals. As the "player," you are the one actually taking the action to make things happen.

Professional athletes have a coach, and I think almost everyone could benefit from this type of leadership and direction. In fact, I've heard that Tiger Woods has four coaches, and Magic Johnson once had six. These elite athletes understand that they can't make their way to the top alone.

Coaching has had a huge impact on the people's lives with whom I've worked. Coaching makes a world of difference to professional athletes and can do the same for individuals and business professionals.

Making great strides toward achieving your goals is empowering. You will feel wonderful with the inevitable result of maintaining a more balanced and enjoyable life. You can look at it this way: a coach helps you create your own personal road map to success as you define it and holds you accountable to achieving it.

Wright

So what are some of the obstacles people encounter when trying achieve their goals on their own?

Bachrach

The biggest obstacle people encounter when they are trying to achieve their goals on their own is lack of accountability. When you have only yourself to report to, it's very easy to procrastinate and let things slide. In the words of Scarlett O'Hara, "Tomorrow is another day." Sadly, tomorrow becomes next week, next week becomes next month, and next month eventually becomes never. You think you know what you want, but don't have the will power or determination to actually take the steps necessary to achieve your goals.

Other times, the problem is linked to a lack of alignment between the conscious and subconscious mind. In other words, you're trying to achieve a goal without genuine motivation. If you're not motivated, you'll never accomplish anything.

So the first step in my process is to identify the client's true goals. If the client's goals are not aligned with their true hopes and desires, the chances that they will ultimately achieve that goal are slim. Many times, people set a goal and then spend the majority of their time obsessing over the reasons why they aren't going to achieve that goal or didn't achieve the goal. These constant negative thoughts destroy your chance of achieving your goals. The subconscious mind is a very powerful tool. When all of the input that the subconscious mind receives is negative, the subconscious will take this input and tell the conscious mind and the body that the goal is not possible. You'd be surprised at how powerful the effects of this negativity are on goal achievement.

I was recently talking to a friend about working out and losing weight. The last few times I had seen her, she'd been quite enthusiastic about her weight loss goals. However, when I asked her how her fitness regimen was going on this visit, she said, "Oh I gave that up." Up until this point, she'd been continually saying, "I'm really fat, I want to lose weight. I'm going to do something about it now."

When I asked her what had changed, she said she just gave up. I pointed out that losing weight was obviously not that important to her, and guess what? She agreed. She said, "You're right. I'm really not willing to do the work so I guess I'm okay with where I am now."

I think a lot of people go through life like my friend. She's not totally happy, but she is okay with that. Sometimes people just don't want their goals badly enough to do whatever it takes to achieve them.

When people identify what their true goals are, a floodlight switches on in their life. There's often an epiphany or a moment of truth where they realize that their goals are within reach or that they were aiming for the wrong objectives to begin with. I am then able to help people create a road map for success that is necessary to achieve their goals within a specific timeframe.

Many people have nothing but the best intentions for their personal growth. Sadly, good intentions just aren't always enough.

Wright

So how is it that when we have good intentions, we still don't always do what we think we want to do?

Bachrach

Wouldn't it be great if our "good intentions" worked the way that we think they should? Unfortunately, not even enthusiasm guarantees positive results. There's often a wide gap between our intentions and our actions. Poor follow-through—consciously deciding to do something, but then not doing it for whatever reason—is simply a fact of life for many of us. We fail to take the action necessary to be in alignment with our good intentions. This can be very frustrating. Poor follow-through can have an effect on virtually every aspect of our lives. This not only threatens our health, but also prevents us from achieving personal, financial, relationship, and career goals that are easily within our reach.

Good intentions don't magically produce good results. They are a start; however, they are unfortunately not enough. Here's the bottom line: An accountability coach holds you accountable to follow through with your "good intentions." No-nonsense encouragement can help you stay focused on your goals, making your odds of succeeding much more likely.

The problem many people face is this: we correlate our past successes with the actions we used to achieve that success. Almost all of us base past successes on past actions. In theory, that line of thinking makes sense. We know what has worked before, so we presume it will work again. Sometimes we are aware that we are doing this and sometimes we are not.

The actions that you used to reach a previous goal will not always work for a new goal. As an accountability coach, I analyze past and present activity against current goals. Albert Einstein summarized this line of thinking best when he said, "Insanity is doing the same thing over and over again and expecting different results." How true that is.

Wright

So how do you hold clients accountable to the activities they know they need to do?

Bachrach

I help people hold themselves accountable to the tasks they know they need to accomplish but don't complete for whatever reason. First, we establish the connection between completing the task and how the work will contribute to their goals. Then I help them set realistic schedules and deadlines. We work together to create structure to track the required milestones, stay laser focused, and work only on the highest payoff activities. We decide what work can be accomplished in the timeframe they established. They calendar everything. There is an effective way to schedule everything in your life that you need to do and it is very important to utilize this method of calendaring and then honor your calendar.

Then we discuss delegation. Truthfully, people should spend their time doing only the things that they enjoy and excel at. The quickest way to accomplish your goals is to focus only on the highest pay-off activities. Everything else should be delegated to someone else or dropped from your life entirely. Now, this is not an option for everyone. However, sometimes I can help people find ways they've never thought of to delegate, delay, or eliminate their burdensome tasks, which allows them to better focus on the things that are most important. My goal is to remove all of the obstacles from your path to success. Sometimes this requires hard choices and sacrifice, but, as you would guess, the payoff is always well worth any pain.

One of the biggest benefits of working with me versus trying to accomplish goals alone is that when we are left to our own devices most of us tend to procrastinate or let ourselves off the hook too easily. Or, the reverse happens and we expect too much. People who are too hard on themselves often set unrealistic goals or deadlines, and then they have no idea how to go about achieving these objectives. They think, "I really want to accomplish this, and I'm trying to accomplish this, so why isn't working?" Then they get frustrated with their lack of progress and give up all together.

I don't think I've ever met a true overachiever, though. I meet people who have big goals and aspirations, but these goals are usually centered on one area of their life. That's why I make everyone have a goal for each of the eight areas on the "Wheel of Life" exercise they initially complete as homework. Balance is essential to your quality of life. You can't be truly happy if you are succeeding in your career and failing in your personal life.

Unfortunately, our good intentions don't always create action. When we do act on our good intentions and start moving in a positive direction, in short a matter of time, many of us find we often start to slip and revert back to our old ways. Forming positive new habits and breaking free from your former lifestyle can be hard, and the whole process takes time. Setbacks are only natural. That's another reason why an accountability coach is so crucial to monumental success. My job is to keep you focused and on track when you lose sight of your goals, and to keep you moving in the right direction.

Having a professional accountability coach in your life to guide you and help you follow through with your good intentions can turn those intentions into the results you truly desire.

Wright

So what happens when the positive feelings associated with working toward your goals isn't enough to keep moving forward?

Bachrach

Well, as an absolute last resort, I will implement a system of consequences for not following through on objectives. For instance, I had one client who said his goal was to improve his social life. This man was a complete workaholic. He had no social life because he never left the office. We created a goal for him to leave the office every day by 6 PM. Well, after a few weeks of his staying well past six o'clock every night, I asked him to tell me what he hated the most in life. What was something that he just couldn't stand? His answer? Cats. So I mailed him a pledge certificate to the Siamese Rescue of San Diego. We agreed that every time he left work after six o'clock, he had to mail a $50 donation to the rescue shelter. The client posted the card in a prominent place above his desk, and guess what? The cats have yet to receive a single penny—even though this non-profit really does need the donations. The good news is that he got a social life and got married.

Another client of mine had an appointment that appeared on his to-do list for two weeks in a row. I got tired of seeing him procrastinate completing this seemingly simple task. Normally, I would work with the client to evaluate whether or not the item should be dropped from the schedule completely. But in this case, we both knew that the event was mandatory for his profession. So, I asked him to mail me a $5,000 check. I told him that I was going to make a generous donation in his name to a political cause that he did not support. He mailed me the check, and then promptly made reservations for the event and completed the activity in no time, so the check never was cashed.

In a way, my system of consequences is like a "swear jar." When you slip up and drop a bad word, you put a dollar or two in the jar. But my consequences differ from the swear jar in two ways Number one: they are enforced. Clients understand that if they aren't honest with me about their actions, they are only hurting themselves. The second way my consequences are different is that they are not always monetary—at least not strictly monetary. Many times, I find that money is a huge motivator; however, money alone isn't always enough. When you drop a few dollars in the swear jar, you're not really hurting yourself for money—and you know that the money is still yours. Imagine now that you have to give all of the money in your swear jar to your worst enemy. That would be a different story, wouldn't it?

Consequences are not a significant part of my system, though. I've only used consequences three or four times ever. I try to keep things positive because if the client's goals are not enough to inspire him or her, something else is clearly going on. I really don't believe in using threats or other negative motivators to get a client moving. The goals and timeframe should be enough to motivate the client to move forward. Above all else, having a professional coach to be accountable to typically motivates people and keeps them on track.

Wright

How do people respond to this style of coaching and encouragement?

Bachrach

As you might guess, people respond differently to this style of encouragement. I will not go so far as to say that every client enjoys working with me. One-on-one coaching can be very difficult, and is certainly not for everyone. I have seen people crack and quit or burn out because they couldn't handle the intensity of accountability coaching.

In fact, one client said he had nightmares before our sessions. I couldn't believe it. We talked about his goals! How scary could that be? This is why I have a personal "Am I Coachable" free assessment for potential clients on my Web site (see contact information at the end of this chapter). I recommend that anyone interested in the coaching process visit the site and complete the assessment. For instance: Not everyone has "big" goals. Not everyone has the ability to handle the truth about his or her life. Clients have to be able to take advice and seek guidance in order to realize their true potential and achieve the goals they say they want. Prospective clients can also take a free Implementation Index on my Web site to help them determine how self-motivated they currently are. Taking action obviously produces results.

But for the most part, clients thrive from having someone on their side, pushing them to new limits. I'm their cheerleader. However, if I have to, I've been known to fire a few clients. I will stop working with a client when he or she continues to put things off week after week and not make any progress on their goals because they aren't doing the work required to achieve what they say they want. That's just a case of wasting time—mine and theirs. My motto is: "excuses don't count unless you're dead." Don't tell me you've been sick for the last two days when you have had two weeks to make progress. Even the best excuses in the world are just that—excuses. That might sound tough, but the reality is that excuses don't help you achieve your goals. Excuses are nothing but a roadblock on your path to achievement. Luckily, when most people work with me they are serious about their goals and dreams, and I don't have to fire them.

The people I coach stay focused and on track, and they accomplish their goals faster than they ever thought possible. As I've said, many times clients are able to exceed their own expectations with just a little bit of guidance and accountability for their actions. My role in their life is part of their road map to success.

Wright

What are the important elements of a successful coaching relationship?

Bachrach

There are a few qualities essential to a successful coaching relationship. First and foremost, there must be a relationship of trust. Trust is built through honest and direct communication. Sometimes the truth isn't easy to say or hear, but ultimately the truth is better for everyone. Another area I emphasize is belief, which relates to trust in some ways. Belief is such a key component to overall success. Belief in yourself, your abilities, the process, and in your coach will enable you to do anything you set your mind to. You wouldn't believe how much more success you can achieve by believing in what you are doing and being completely into the process.

Expectations are also important. There should be a mutual understanding of the expectations of the relationship that are established early in the relationship. These expectations will guide the relationship and provide forward momentum as I encourage clients to set and achieve their goals, keeping in mind that when necessary, course adjustments are allowed.

In any coaching relationship, a mutual respect is also important. Respect for me is established through the recognition of my experience, knowledge, abilities, attitude, and results, and my sincere care for each of my clients.

Clients should also recognize that a coaching relationship is a partnership with one goal: to help them achieve what they truly desire. The partnership has more power than the individual alone.

The structure of the relationship is established initially through my systems and processes. This structure can later be modified to provide the greatest acceleration of results for each unique client. This balance of rigidity and flexibility produces effective results with the least amount of effort possible.

Finally, I ask all clients to respect the value of time. Each of my one-on-one clients schedules a specific time to talk with me two times per month, based on personal schedules. No time is wasted with excuses and reasons why something didn't get done. We focus on what was done, progress, and what has to be done to reach goals in the timeframe established. Remember my motto: Excuses Don't Count Unless You Are Dead.

The people who benefit the most from my one-on-one or group coaching:

- Have a strong desire to reach the next level and tap into their true potential,
- Are willing to make the sacrifices needed to get to the next level,
- Are dissatisfied with their current level of achievement or the pace,
- Operate with a sense of urgency to accelerate desired results, goals, dreams, and desires,
- Know how to hire and utilize the skills and experience of professionals,
- Want a more balanced life, and want to be able to sustain that life balance.

Wright

So what else do you think stops people from achieving their goals? After all, goal setting seems pretty straightforward.

Bachrach

For starters, we all fear the unknown to some degree. Sometimes our minds become accustomed to striving for an objective and fear the change that is required for us to actually reach our goals.

Fear of loss is more often than not a greater human motivator than the desire to gain. When we operate from a position of fear rather than a position of strength, we impede our own progress. There are usually obstacles between us and our goals. We need courage to overcome many of them.

Sometimes we fail to take action because we don't know how the change will affect our life. Sometimes we fail to take action because we feel comfortable in our current position. Sometimes we fail to take action because we are unsure of how someone might respond to us. There could be any number of reasons that we fail to take action.

Think about people who lose a significant amount of weight. Their change in appearance can alter many factors in their life. People will look at them differently, and others' reactions to them will change. A spouse or friend might become insecure, placing a new kind of stress on the relationship. Even the person's reflection has changed.

A dramatic change in your life can have surprising effects, many of which are unknown when you begin the process of change. This can be frightening. Again, this is fear of outcome. While we cannot control the reactions of other people, we can surmise the possible outcomes and be prepared.

Someone wise once said, "You will remain the same until the pain of remaining the same becomes greater than the pain it takes to change."

Preparation breeds the confidence to take action. Part of my system involves motivating people to take action to discover other peoples' reactions and results. When people are pleasantly surprised with outcomes, they are "on fire" to take more actions.

Accountability coaching provides checks at intervals to prepare for the next action and addresses fears.

Wright

What specific things do you do when you begin working with a client?

Bachrach

We begin with the premise that accountability coaching is really about quality of life. Of course, a person's quality of life has many different aspects. I start with the Wheel of Life, which has been around for a very long time and actually is used by many different coaches in various ways. I use the wheel to identify eight areas of a client's life with the goal of creating balance in all eight areas.

The areas of my wheel include career, money, fitness and health, family and friends, romance/partner, personal growth and spiritual development, fun and recreation, and physical environment. I ask clients to rank each area of their life on a scale of one to ten, with ten being ideal or excellent and one being dismal. Then we primarily determine how to improve the areas that are lacking.

Understand that coaching should not improve one area at the expense of other areas. If your professional life is outstanding, but your personal life is lacking, we don't take away the elements that make your professional life successful in order to improve your personal life. Coaching is all about balance. I work with people so that they don't have to sacrifice one area that is really good to bring one area that isn't as good up to a higher level of satisfaction and fulfillment.

The goal of the wheel of life is to gauge where the client is right now and improve upon that. Any of my clients can easily assess where they are right now on their Wheel of Life by going to my Web site and using the automated version of this exercise. They can then reassess where they are as time goes on with where they are in each of the eight areas.

Clients set *at least* one goal for each of the eight areas of their Wheel of Life. For instance, I recently began working with a woman who had just gone through a divorce. She said she really wasn't ready for dating yet, but because romance/partner is a component of the wheel of life, she had to come up with at least one goal for this area. The goal might be something as simple as deciding to take a step to meet eligible men. She doesn't necessarily have to jump headfirst into the dating pool; she just needs to take a step in the right direction to improve that area of her life on a short-term basis. She took the small step and is now dating a wonderful man. Things happen when we are open to the notion.

Wright

How does the Wheel of Life approach to goal-setting affect one's overall quality of life?

Bachrach

As a matter of fact, the affect can be quite dramatic. The results of this newfound balance shock and amaze my clients as well as their family and friends. Many of my clients are men. They'll say, "My wife loves you so much," and I've never even met or talked with their wife. Even if the client's coaching began with the intent to improve his or her business, the affects spread into the personal side of the person's life. I hear clients say, "I have more time with my wife. We go on real dates—dates that are her idea of a date, not mine. I'm actually losing weight, I'm happier, I have more time off, and somehow I'm making more money too."

In fact, many of my clients see their revenue improve at least 20 percent yearly and some a lot more, and they have a more balanced life. As someone once said, "If you always do what you always did, you'll always get what you always got."

My goal is to help my clients make their Wheel of Life as round as possible for a smooth ride on the road map to success as opposed to continually riding a rollercoaster.

We reevaluate clients' responses to the categories of the wheel at least yearly to gauge their progress and see what types of adjustments should be made to their goals. We also reevaluate responses when clients are going through a significant transition in their life. The goal is to constantly be aware of where clients are ranking themselves at the moment in order to accelerate results.

I get a great sense of satisfaction and fulfillment when I see a client use the road map to success systems I've created to reach his or her goals. Seeing people who were seemingly stuck in one place suddenly make exciting advances in their life is unbelievably rewarding. I have helped many people exceed their own ideas of their potential. Using these systems and creating your game plan is like creating your personal road map to success.

Another powerful tool clients enjoy is the Quality of Life Enhancer® exercise, created by Bill Bachrach, Bachrach & Associates, Inc. So often we make choices about how we'll spend our time unconsciously, and this exercise is designed to help you make conscious choices about things that are important to you. You'll find this fun and thought-provoking on-line exercise at my Web site, at no charge. Feel free to share this exercise with anyone.

I think a large part of the reason I enjoy coaching so much is because clients are active participants in their own transformation. My clients want to improve their lives. That's why they contacted me in the first place. Clients know that they want to improve their quality of life across the board, and they know that hard work will be required. They just don't know how to take the next step. Many times, they've been struggling for years to achieve their goals with very little progress. Their lack of success in the past is not always correlated with a lack of effort. Sometimes it's as simple as having someone like me in their life to help them stay focused on the "right" activities and someone who cares about their success.

When you have someone in your corner you can speak with on a regular basis, you can make great strides on your journey toward balance and achievement.

Wright

How do you meet with your clients?

Bachrach

Coaching can be effective in a number of different venues. Almost all of my coaching, however, is completed entirely via e-mail and phone. I rarely meet my clients in person; in fact, I have no idea what many of them look like. All that matters is their belief in themselves, dedication to the process, and their desire for the outcome. During coaching calls, there's no small talk or chitchat because there isn't time and it isn't important to the outcome. I'm direct, and I tell the truth as I see it. This ability allows me to provide insight and clarity into someone's life and goals in a very direct and truthful manner. My role is to help people put the pieces of their life together so that they can find balance and move forward in their personal development.

Clients send me a report the day before our scheduled phone call. They create the reports themselves, based on a sample I initially send them. Many of my forms are Excel worksheets used as tracking mechanisms. When I receive the report, I evaluate the client's progress on their objectives. I have a knack for looking at things and seeing the holes or disconnects, and then asking a lot of thought-provoking questions.

When I see one of these disconnects, I'll address the issue directly with a client. I'll ask something like: if you did this, how come this didn't occur? For instance, I noticed that one client had met with seventeen clients, yet had no referrals.

During our conversation, I asked him, "How is that possible? You had seventeen great opportunities!"

His reply: "I just didn't ask for a variety of reasons."

My job is to figure out exactly what has been holding my clients back, and come up with a new strategy to help them achieve the desired outcome. My one-on-one coaching is entirely customized based on the accuracy of their reports.

Wright

What do you think holds people back from hiring an accountability coach?

Bachrach

The whole concept of coaching still has an unfamiliar, new-fangled feel for some people. Many people have no idea how powerful coaching can be for their personal and professional life. When people discover the benefits of accountability coaching they become very interested. When people experience the excitement of achieving their goals in less time, they are convinced. Within a very short period of time, they see the difference someone like me makes in their life and things quickly start to happen. It is a great feeling for them to see the impact this relationship has on their personal and professional life, and it is a great feeling for me to see people realizing their true potential and achieving goals they dreamed about achieving.

As with all ventures, people act when they realize the value of what they are receiving will equal or outweigh what they are sacrificing. Putting aside your inhibitions and doubts is a small price to pay for the remarkable change you will experience in your quality of life.

Wright

I'm curious—what are some of the successes that your clients enjoy as a result of working with you?

Bachrach

Most clients experience similar results because we are working on quality of life and life balance in the same eight areas with each person.

One of my clients said: *"I originally signed on with Anne to help me get more focused on my business, and yes she has helped me do that. But the biggest value I have gotten from her is in my quality of life. My marriage is better, my physical health is better, I am more focused on the spiritual aspects of my life, my relationships with my children and friends are better, and I am just having more fun than ever before!"*

Another one of my clients said: *"In the time I have worked with Anne, which was only six months, she helped me change not only my business, but my life. With her help, no-excuses attitude, and amazing ability to see through the fog of my own distractions, I not only achieved one of the goals I was most afraid to set, but I actually exceeded it. My personal life has flourished because my professional life has structure and boundaries. Through objective questioning and a judgment-free attitude, Anne helped me discover what I really want out of my life."*

One client recently said: *"I hired Anne as my coach to help me develop and execute a plan that would give me financial freedom and create a rewarding everyday life. Her process has completely restructured the way I focus my attention so I can achieve my goals. I am amazed how her coaching has streamlined my plan in only a few months. She has a unique gift to help others achieve their highest potential."*

Clients I coach typically report:

- More clarity, focus, and direction,
- Less procrastination and fewer stops,
- Achievement of results they only dreamed possible,
- Enhanced and more satisfying relationships,
- Increased income, and
- A more balanced and fulfilling life.

Wright

Do you have any additional thoughts for our readers?

Bachrach

When you really think about it, what do you ultimately want your professional and personal life to be like? What does your Wheel of Life look like with tens in each section? Working with a coach or coaches can have a big impact on your life and allows you to obtain what you really want from life.

What got you to where you are now may not be effective in getting you to where you want to be in the future. You may have to get creative to move to your next level—and we all have a next level. Most of us just can't do it alone when we are left to our own devices. If you aren't on the path to achieving all your goals in the timeframe you have established and you would truly like to achieve your goals, desires, and dreams, fulfill what's important to you, and experience an even better quality of life, then working with a coach or coaches might be the most important experience you'll ever have.

Wright

Well, what a great conversation. I've learned a lot here today about accountability coaching and creating a balanced life, and I'm sure our readers will as well. Anne, I really appreciate all this time you've taken to answer these questions and spending so much time with me here today on such an important and interesting topic.

Bachrach

It's been my pleasure, David. I appreciate your interest.

Wright

Today we've been talking with Anne Bachrach. She is President of A.M. Enterprises, a California-based life-coaching firm. For nearly a quarter of a century she has worked to help businesspeople and entrepreneurs improve their productivity, profitability, and quality of life. Her coaching is in high demand and she only works, by her own admission, with clients who are truly serious about achieving all their goals and living their dreams. It sounds to me as though she's really serious about helping them.

Anne, thank you so much for being with us today on *Road Map to Success.*

Bachrach

Thank you, David. Much continued success to you.

About the Author

Anne Bachrach has twenty-three years of experience training and coaching. Anne works to help businesspeople and entrepreneurs improve their productivity, profitability, and quality of life. Through her proven systems, she inspires her clients to stay focused and take action on the highest payoff activities that lead to their ultimate professional and personal success. Bachrach's fresh approach to business and life offers a much needed boost for stagnant businesses. She believes that even the most motivated people need accountability to achieve their highest potential. By utilizing her powerful processes, Anne's clients learn how to maximize their talents and bring balance to their lives. Her coaching is in high demand and she only works with clients who are truly serious about achieving all of their goals and living their dreams.

Anne Bachrach
A.M. Enterprises
885 La Jolla Corona Ct.
La Jolla, CA 92037-7445
Phone: 858.456.0160
Fax: 858.456.0158
Anne@AccountabilityCoach.com
www.AccountabilityCoach.com

ROADMAP to SUCCESS 6

An interview with...

Angela DeFinis

David Wright (Wright)

I am speaking today with Angela DeFinis, Founder and President of DeFinis Communications, Inc., a San Francisco Bay Area based presentation skills training company founded in 1997.

Angela DeFinis is an industry expert in presentation skills and speaker coaching. She has spent over twenty years helping business professionals communicate with greater poise, power, and passion. Using her signature Line by Line Coaching™ process Ms. DeFinis and her talented staff have trained business leaders and other professionals to speak with increased skill and confidence in engaging any audience. A "gifted coach," Angela's compassion and energy create an environment where every individual can fully discover the elegance and power of successfully communicating with others. Her focus is in helping speakers do just one thing—come alive!

Welcome to *Roadmap to Success*.

Angela DeFinis

Thank you, David. It is a pleasure to be a part of this project.

There was an article in *Fortune* magazine a few months ago that highlighted four key skills required for career advancement and business success: remembering names, speed-reading, negotiation skills and, at the top of the list, public speaking.

So I know this topic is an important one for our readers. I hope this information will help our readers become better communicators and as a result gain success in business and in life.

Wright

It's good to have your expertise with us on this topic. Before we learn more about your specific methods for helping people succeed in this important skill area, I think our readers will appreciate learning more about you. What drew you to the subject of public speaking and communication skills in the first place? What was your career path?

DeFinis

Well, I had good fortune in this area in my early life. I grew up in a restaurant family in Washington, D.C. As a teenager I spent every summer working as a waitress in one of my parents' restaurants. During those years I was surrounded by people for whom persuasive speech was a way of life. Our "regular" customers were such distinguished politicians as former Speaker of the House Thomas "Tip" O'Neill, Representative Gillespie V. "Sonny" Montgomery, and the legendary Robert C. Byrd. These people were among the great communicators of their era and I had the opportunity to see them in action in a very informal setting. There they were, eating spaghetti and garlic bread and comfortably communicating with ease and skill—telling stories, creating relationships, and so naturally engendering trust in those around them. Their ability to communicate seemed effortless to me.

I remember many nights when Tip O'Neill would stay late and he and my father would sit together at a corner table telling stories until midnight. It was exciting to witness.

I realized that these magnanimous personalities also used their communication skills to set legislative policy. They made the world a better place and had a positive impact on the lives of millions of people. That left a very strong impression on me.

But I was drawn to these statesmen not because they were people with power and authority, but because they were warm, funny, sincere, friendly, and alive! And this is what I try to have my clients understand—to be a good communicator you have to cultivate these very personal skills above all. You have to clearly demonstrate to others that you sincerely enjoy the communication process and that you care about them—that you are alive!

I majored in English in college and loved the theatre. Before going to graduate school I spent several years on stage. I was an actress with a touring reader's theater company and that's where I learned about stage presence, the power of vocal resonance, and how to reach an audience with greater precision and command. I also went to clown school at one point, which in addition to adding a great deal to my personal communication style, has also provided a wealth of stories over the years.

My transition to the corporate world came as a result of my own search for career change—and some good luck. I took classes in career development at a major training company and was asked to become a trainer for them. I worked in the corporate classroom teaching career development, communication, sales, and leadership skills. The common thread that ran throughout each class was always "persuasive communication."

After many years learning the ropes of the training business and refining my skills, I set out on my own and founded DeFinis Communications. Through it all I realized the critical role that good communication— specifically good presentation skills—had in the lives of those I worked with. I am passionate about helping people achieve success in this important area.

Wright

From clown school to the corporate world—you have quite an interesting background. With all your experience over the years, what do you find to be the greatest challenge people face when giving presentations?

DeFinis

It is well documented that people fear speaking in public more than just about anything. These days there is a long list of fears out there from terrorist activity to bird flu to global warming, and yes, even though the list is long, public speaking remains the number one fear of mankind. We fear it more than death.

I see this fear rear its ugly head with my clients in the form of extreme physical unrest and mental paralysis. I call it "The Big Freeze." When I ask people what this feels like for them I hear such things as, "My words never make it out of my mouth—they get stuck in the back of my throat." Or, "I just can't think clearly, I never know what's coming next." Or, "I feel like my heart is beating outside my shirt and everyone can see it." Or, "When I know my topic I'm great—when I don't I freeze."

These kinds of feelings do get in the way of being a competent, persuasive communicator and I feel great compassion for people who have these types of responses. I worked with a civil engineer recently who gives software product demonstrations for a living. He confessed that on a scale of one to ten (with ten being the worst possible feeling of fear when speaking to a group), he rated himself a twenty-five! And this is someone with a lot of experience, whose job requires that he speak to groups several times a week. What I found truly amusing though, was that for "fun" this man liked to skydive. Can you imagine? There is nothing on this earth that would compel me to jump out of an airplane for "fun."

Wright

I'm with you on that one. It sounds like people bring all sorts of challenges your way.

DeFinis

Yes, some days I think I've heard it all and then some days I'm stunned at what people reveal. I received a call a few years ago from a marketing VP at a major entertainment company. He said he traveled all over the world speaking on behalf of the company and needed help with his presentation skills.

I asked him to send a tape of a recent speech and what I saw surprised me. Here was a man who was as poised and polished as anyone I've seen. Articulate and engaging, he had a certain charm that was compelling. He also had very good technique so I could tell he had been well coached.

When I spoke to him on the phone and mentioned his obvious polish and skill he still insisted on meeting. So, we met and what he said was this: "I know I'm a good speaker but I suffer from extreme nervousness before every speech. I can't give a presentation without first going into the men's room and throwing up."

I had read about people—famous people—who did this, but I had never worked with anyone who struggled in this way. I was fortunate to have the tools, techniques, and resources to help him overcome his severe reaction. We worked together for several months and over time he greatly improved. It thrills me that I still get a Christmas card from him every year. He tells me he's composed and relaxed when he speaks now. And he always signs the card, "Thank you for changing my life."

Wright

That must be gratifying.

DeFinis

Yes, extremely.

Wright

Why do you think this happens to experienced presenters like your civil engineer and marketing VP?

DeFinis

I find that most people are gripped with fear because they don't know what it takes to give a presentation. They "talk" every day of their lives, so they think the same communication skills apply to giving a presentation; when those skills don't work they panic. There is a huge gap between what they think they need to do and what is actually required of them in the role of speaker—and that gap is unfortunately filled with fear.

Once they learn the unique components of persuasive presentations, the fear subsides and the gap is filled in with concrete knowledge, practical skill, tools for audience engagement, and a deeper understanding of the communication process.

Wright

How do you help people overcome these challenges and fill in the gap? When someone wants to improve his or her public speaking skills, where is the best place to start?

DeFinis

Well, the best place to start is with a basic understanding of what is required when giving a presentation.

Let's look at this comparison: Imagine that you are sitting at a conference table—or the dinner table, for that matter—with six or seven people. Each person contributes to the conversation in an easy, natural way. One person might ask a question, one person gives detailed information on the topic at hand, another tells a story or gives an example, and someone else makes a joke. You can see that the conversation has a lot of dynamic movement, which creates a certain momentum. It's like watching a well-played soccer game when the ball is "passed" effortlessly from player to player in an attempt to reach the goal.

This type of conversation, where everyone at the table is contributing, helps each person stay involved with the group and the subject. The group is connected tightly or loosely around a topic, a task, a value, a philosophy, a specific outcome, or just for enjoyment. Except for the most introverted among us this is an easy form of communication. The group holds the key to group connection and knowledge transfer. It happens naturally. We have a lot of experience with this type of communication because we've done it all our lives.

Now, what if we take one person—let's call her Jane—out of this comfortable group and ask her to stand up and *give a presentation*. If we stick with our soccer analogy this is like taking a penalty kick. Instead of being able to pass the ball to another team member to keep the game moving, Jane is facing the goal all alone. There is no team to help her move the ball—it's all up to her. In a presentation there is a shift as well. The group is now an audience—expectant, listening. The shared conversation has shifted and the responsibility lies *solely* with Jane. Now it is up to her to keep the group connected and involved. Jane, not the group, holds the key to knowledge transfer. It is up to her to share the data, give an example, create a metaphor, tell a story, ask a question, or use any number of communication techniques and rhetorical devices to keep the group involved and make the communication come alive.

This ability to keep the audience engaged so that knowledge can be powerfully transferred is what we call The Connection Loop. One key principle of The Connection Loop is this: the speaker (in this case Jane) is *solely* responsible for the audience's experience.

Wright

That is a lot of responsibility for one person. No wonder we are all intimidated by the prospect of public speaking. Tell our readers more about your model.

DeFinis

I'd love to. When you ask me where we start in helping a speaker overcome fear—it is with The Connection Loop. Once you realize that your job as a speaker involves much more than just putting your PowerPoint slides together on the fly, you can begin the process of acquiring the skills to actually *do* the job instead of fretting about it.

Structure is the key. Our model outlines what is required for every speaker to succeed. It defines the speaker's unique role and responsibilities. And this is usually a big relief to our clients. Once they understand that being in the role of speaker requires that they actually take charge and *lead,* we can get right to work in learning the skills to help them perform effectively. We quickly move away from the words "fear," "stuck," and "freeze" and into the words, "action" "involvement," and "energy."

Wright

What do our readers need to do to keep an audience involved and engaged?

DeFinis

They need to learn a simple process that they can quickly adopt and use. There are two key elements that insure the audience stays engaged. The first is a speaker's *performance* and the second is the speaker's *content.*

Let's start with performance. I like to use a metaphor from the natural world to help us understand how a speaker's performance keeps an audience engaged. When you think of the creation of fire, for example, there are three elements that must be present for fire to ignite and burn: heat, fuel, and oxygen. These elements are required to create and sustain a flame. If you remove any one of these elements the fire will eventually die out.

I love the fire metaphor because there is a similar phenomenon that occurs when giving a presentation. There are three key ingredients that must be present to light a fire in an audience: a speaker's body, voice, and words. These are your *performance* skills. How you engage an audience with your body, voice, and words has a big impact on your success. And like a fire, if you remove any one of these ingredients you will reduce your energy, and the connection between you and your audience will diminish. We've all seen this happen—we've seen speakers lose energy and like a fire, "die out" right in front of our eyes.

So, when we look at how speakers manage to keep an audience engaged and alive throughout an *entire* presentation we have to look at how they maintain their *performance* skills. We think of this as having the ability to "Create Performance Combustion." This is our core performance model. It insures that you and your audience stay in the "Connection Loop."

Wright

Will you tell us more about these performance skills?

DeFinis

Yes. I see the skills in these three categories as crucial to any speaker's ability to engage an audience. Helping people develop these skills is an exciting part of my job. Let's take a look at each one:

Physical Presence: This is what the audience sees when they look at you. Imagine that they can't hear a word you are saying. The only information they have available is the physical information you are sending to them with your *body language*. The skills you rely on to establish and maintain physical presence are your non-verbal skills: eye contact, facial expression, posture, gestures, and movement.

Vocal Resonance: Your vocal presence is the creation and delivery of your *vocal sounds*. Imagine that no one in the audience can see you—that their eyes are closed and they only have access to your message through your voice. How do you keep your audience engaged and connected? The skills that help you do this include: volume, enunciation, pronunciation, rate of speech, pitch, inflection, and strategic pauses.

Distinctive Language: Your *words* give people direct access to your message and help keep your audience stimulated and involved. The skills you can use to be engaging and credible include: crafting concise sentences, selecting language that is audience-focused, and liberally using words that convey power and emotion. It's also important to eliminate distracting words such as: really, like, basically, okay, you know, and it is equally important to drop non-words from your delivery such as: um, ah, er, and uh. Keep your language clear and free of word pollution.

To be an effective communicator with the capacity to create a fire in the belly of your audience, all three of these elements must be ignited and maintained.

I recently worked with a woman who has been in radio for fifteen years. She now wants to take her message to a different audience and speak to groups. As you can imagine, she has excellent Vocal Resonance. Her voice is highly trained, proficient in range, clear, varied, and confident.

But her highly sophisticated vocal skill does not naturally transfer to the area of Physical Presence. She has little physical poise—her posture is slumped, her gestures are repetitive, she has limited torso movement, and she rarely smiles or raises her eyebrows. She stands in one place and lets that beautiful voice do all the work—as though no one can see her! And that makes complete sense given that she has spent fifteen years behind a microphone never thinking about the impact of her physical presence.

It has been a pleasure working with her because she is an eager and responsive professional who pays attention to the details and learns quickly. I can readily see when the light goes on and she "gets" what I'm asking of her. Her determination to improve her physical presence is an inspiration and her hard work is paying off. She is becoming a stronger, more physically poised and polished speaker every day.

So, for those who aspire to be great speakers—to move an audience in a meaningful way and transfer knowledge with elegance and power—this ability to Create Performance Combustion is crucial. Cultivating the skills of

Physical Presence, Vocal Resonance, and Distinctive Language will quickly accelerate your speaking power.

Wright

You just mentioned the woman with the great radio voice. I have always been aware of the power of voice. Tell us more about the importance of Vocal Resonance in giving a presentation.

DeFinis

Yes, what is it about the voice that compels people in such a powerful way? Think about the voices of great speakers like John F. Kennedy, Martin Luther King, Winston Churchill, and Franklin D. Roosevelt. Once you've heard those voices you never forget them. It's as if the voice alone is capable of carrying the message into eternity. To achieve that kind of vocal vitality the key is *liberation*—freeing the voice so that it can fluidly move the message with passion and elegance. My clients are subject matter experts. They are intensely passionate about their topics but often unable to express their passion because their voices have so little range and power.

I worked with a sales executive recently who faced this dilemma. He was speaking at his company's annual worldwide kick-off meeting and needed to motivate his large sales staff. He had been with the company for a long time, had extensive knowledge of, and experience with its products and services. He felt deep passion and excitement, but he couldn't show it. He was low key, a bit too informal, and concerned about sounding "fake and insincere."

Helping him make critical adjustments to his vocal resonance changed everything for him. When he stood up at the meeting and gave his presentation, he spoke with great pride and passion—and the sales force actually cheered! I always make it a point to spend considerable time with my clients on vocal awareness and skill building and I recommend that our readers do the same. It pays to liberate your voice.

Let's look more closely at Vocal Resonance and the power of the voice. There are three key areas to consider that will help you develop strong vocal skills:

Vocal Clarity is the ease with which a listener can understand what you are saying. Nothing is more frustrating for an audience than listening to a speaker and barely understanding every third or fourth word because of a soft voice, mumbling, or poor pronunciation. The listener doesn't want to work that hard. The skills that help you achieve vocal clarity include: volume, enunciation, and pronunciation.

Vocal Variety is the interest you generate in your listeners when you produce changes in various vocal characteristics, such as your rate of speech and pitch. You express your attitude toward your topic (and your audience) when you use vocal variety to express the range and depth of your emotion. You can sound at different times excited, enthusiastic, serious, and knowledgeable just by your tone of voice. The skills that help you achieve vocal variety include: rate of speech and pitch.

Vocal Emphasis is the way in which you accent syllables, words, and silence to stress importance and to give meaning to our sentences. We achieve vocal emphasis when we use proper inflection and strategic pauses. Using these skills helps the audience to understand what you think is important and meaningful about your message.

Wright

If you had to choose just one Vocal Resonance skill that our readers should practice immediately, what would it be?

DeFinis

All of these skills are important for achieving strong Vocal Resonance, but if there is one skill to immediately add to your repertoire it is the "strategic pause." The word "pause" comes from the Greek word, *pauein,* meaning "stop." I suggest that we take this literally and do exactly that. Stop talking after *every second or third word.* You might think this sounds crazy—and it does take some getting used to—but it works! Everyone I work with comes across as more powerful and confident the second they slow down and pause—and the side benefit is that speaking at a slower pace allows for longer, deeper breathing to calm the nervous system. It's a big win for the audience and a big win for the speaker. So, the one formula to keep in mind is this: P = P (Pause equals Power). When in doubt, heed the advice of the Greeks.

Wright

I know our readers are intrigued by the concept of Creating Performance Combustion and the physical and vocal elements of effective speaking. What about the content? What do you recommend for message development?

DeFinis

Content development is equally important of course. If having the ability to Create Performance Combustion gives us a formula for "how" one delivers a presentation, our second model—the DeFinis Navigator—lays out the requirements for "what" is being delivered. These are two sides of the same coin and completely interdependent.

The DeFinis Navigator is a content design tool. It provides a method for organizing your message and helps you and your listeners stay on track. By organizing the sections of your talk into distinct parts, the information you share is easier for the audience to follow and digest. This structure is also helpful for the speaker. It's the cure for the "I can't keep my thoughts straight" challenge.

So, let's take a look at how to structure your content. The DeFinis Navigator has a few fundamental components. The first is audience analysis. Once you know your audience, then you can begin to organize your content into three categories: The Opening, The Body, and The Close.

Analyze Your Audience: The first step is *to analyze* who is in your audience so that you understand more about their needs. You'll want to understand the logistics of the situation as well as the profile of the people in the group. Ask questions like: What is the make-up of this group? How many are familiar with my subject? How many equal or surpass my expertise? What do they need from me? These types of questions will provide a guideline for creating your content

Once you have Analyzed Your Audience then you can begin to structure your message with The Opening, The Body, and The Close. It's funny how such a simple model as this can be so enlightening to our clients. Most of us learned this type of message structure in sixth grade, but we don't think of applying it to our presentations; yet, it is essential.

The Opening: We all know that the presentation can be won or lost in the first few minutes. Your intent is to gain immediate attention, provide an outline of the main points to be covered, and establish your credibility. This will keep your audience in the Connection Loop from the start. The opening has four parts: The hook, the introduction, the purpose, and the agenda. Each one of these plays an important role in setting the stage for your presentation.

The Body: The body of your presentation constitutes about 70 percent of your talk. So it's important to have a method for organizing all that information, otherwise it may be overwhelming for you and the audience. I'm a big fan of chunking things down into small manageable parts, so you want to make sure that you have no more than three to five main points. I think of each main point as a "mini" presentation—each should be able to stand alone.

Each main point must be supported by a series of "Touch Points." These can include stories, anecdotes, analogies, quotes, rhetorical questions, examples, technical information, facts, statistics, charts, graphs, visuals—and humor. The point is to "touch" your audience intellectually and emotionally throughout your presentation. The more you are able to expand your use of these resources the greater your ability to persuade and engage.

I work with many technical professionals; in fact, we have a niche in the software industry. As you may know, the engineering community is notorious for spewing content and data like a fire hose. It is easy for technical presenters to get caught up in this type of data explosion. These are serious subject matter experts and they feel a great obligation to tell their audiences *every single thing they know* about the topic at hand. But this inability to break up the data with examples, stories, analogies, and other rhetorical tools can cause audience overload and frustration. So, I caution my technical clients to resist the urge to give these kinds of "data only" presentations and remember that those "techie" audiences have the same need for high engagement and connection as everyone else. The solution for developing powerful and effective technical presentations is in using a variety of "touch points."

The "Value Point" is the personal or business benefit your main point supplies for your audience. "Value Points" connect the audience to your message and provide a link back to the overall purpose. They also answer the important question on the mind of every audience member: "How will this information help me solve my problem?"

The Close: A strong close recaps the core purpose of your presentation and reclaims lost audience attention. I call it "the close" because in the sales world this phrase indicates that the deal has ended successfully. The close is your final opportunity to persuade your point of view and to make your call to action. An effective close has four key elements: the summary, the Q&A, the thank you, and a final thought.

Transitions: Transitions are important for keeping you and your audience on course and I strongly recommend that you take the time to craft your transitions and *memorize* them. Transitions are the super glue that keeps the message together. If you have developed and memorized your transitions you will always know where you are going, and even in the worst of circumstances stay on track.

Wright

This sounds like a pretty involved process. Does it work for every presentation topic?

DeFinis

Yes, it works for just about any type of presentation. I recently worked with the CEO/Founder of a start-up company. His organization was one of thirteen selected out of two hundred initial competitors to present at a large technical conference to a team of evaluators for venture capital funding. He had exactly *five minutes* to give a product demo.

We used the DeFinis Navigator to build his short demo and didn't cut corners. We outlined, we structured, we developed, we edited, we refined, and ultimately we made every word count. It may have been short but his demo was packed with punch from the opening hook to the final thought. Best of all, his company was awarded the funding.

Wright

In most presentations, stories play an important role. Tell us why you think stories work so well in engaging an audience.

DeFinis

There's no doubt about it, audiences prefer stories. And stories are a powerful way to engage the hearts and minds of your listeners. One of the reasons that stories work so well in engaging an audience is because the audience sees a familiar story structure—one they know in their bones. The phrases "let me tell you a story" or "listen to this" or "I heard a great story last week" set the stage for a familiar communication pattern that we have heard all our lives. We expect a pearl of wisdom to follow such a phrase, so we pay attention and listen more intently. We believe we just might hear something new and important—a message that will help us solve one of life's many mysteries. And who can resist that?

A good story not only creates a familiar framework for your message, but it also stimulates a strong emotional connection between you and the audience. Stories that tap our emotions can add a whole new level to the typical talking head who reads every line of a PowerPoint presentation verbatim. Tell a story and you become audience-focused. Tell a story and you become approachable. Tell a story and you *connect*.

Wright

In addition to being personal and entertaining, what other roles do stories play?

DeFinis

Stories play many different roles in a presentation. One of the ways that stories function is as gatekeepers. Stories filter out the less critical information so that our best ideas come shining through. We're all struggling with information overload. As the information mounts up, we strain to manage it all. We become saturated and easily lose sight of what deserves our immediate attention and action.

So how do we sift through the wave of information that inundates us every day? One way we do this is by telling stories. Stories are a microcosm of life. They present just one key theme, one action line, one small group of characters. Stories keep life simple.

The second way that stories function is to unify and motivate us to work more effectively together. Today's workforce doesn't want to be told what to think and how to do what they're supposed to do. This type of prescriptive approach often creates resistance and conflict. A healthy workforce requires cooperation rather than competition. So how do we influence others and encourage individuals and teams to collaborate and work more powerfully together? We do this by creating a story that unifies and motivates. A good story, told with sincerity and intelligence, has the power to do this.

Finally, stories teach the fundamentals. For centuries our oral traditions have influenced the way we think and behave, including our cultural norms and moral beliefs, and the activities of daily life. Stories helped us learn how to plant seeds and raise farm animals, participate in religious ceremonies, and engage in educational opportunities. Stories have played a big cultural role in keeping people motivated to achieve their goals and create productive and healthy societies. All organizations and individuals can use storytelling to teach and frame culture, values, beliefs, and norms in much the same way that stories have been used for centuries. It is exciting to be able to carry on this powerful oral tradition and I encourage my clients and our readers to add meaningful stories to every presentation.

Wright

You have worked with many different speakers in your career. What are some of your coaching secrets?

DeFinis

I work with all types of speakers from C level and senior executives to sales professionals, engineering professionals, and individual contributors to authors who are going on book tours to professional speakers who are on the circuit, teachers, ministers, eighth grade graduation speakers—everyone who speaks.

The process I have developed after years of thought, experience, and polish is a method I call Line by Line Coaching™. This is my signature coaching approach and its success relies on just one thing: the capacity of both teacher and student to be *fully present* and committed to the coaching process.

Imagine that you and I are working together on a presentation you will be giving. Our first step is to establish a benchmark. We get you "on camera" and review your existing strengths and areas for growth. Once we have a game plan we begin the exciting Line by Line Coaching™ process. And it is exciting! We take just one line of your presentation material and fully explore its potential. That means you may be repeating and re-working this line for several minutes or longer until we get it right. I keep one eye on the detail of the moment—the technique and the craft—and the other eye on the big picture—the vision of your success. That gives you, the student, a lot of support and freedom to stay focused in *your* moment, to concentrate on the specific practice and not worry about the big picture. I think it's the role that any good coach plays—to help the student stay focused and concentrate, even when it's tiring and difficult. The discipline, support, and compassion of a master coach help speakers improve and excel.

The Line by Line Coaching™ process can be intense and demanding but it achieves powerful results. I had one client tell me that it was more difficult than having open-heart surgery! But he also said that like his surgery, he felt great afterward and that the coaching was the best he'd ever had.

So, why do I use such a rigorous learning method? Because I believe that one single line holds the very essence of your message and delivery. One line contains the spirit of your entire presentation and getting it right is our greatest goal. This approach accelerates the performance of every presenter at every level so he or she becomes confident and competent in all types of communication—formal or informal—whether on the main stage, at a staff meeting, or at the dinner table.

Wright

What is your greatest hope for your clients and all those who aspire to be more confident and competent public speakers?

DeFinis

My greatest hope is that they will one day feel completely unencumbered in sharing their passion and expertise in front of a group. Whether it's a company meeting, a product demonstration to a small group, a main stage motivational speech, or a sermon on Sunday morning, I want them to fully understand and embrace their unique and important role and perform at will—not because of ego or pride, but because they have an essential right to be in that role and the communication skills to support it. I want them to know that their message is important and needs to be heard. If they have the knowledge and experience, then my job is to help them understand that they also have the personal and communication power.

Most people I work with are subject matter experts and very successful at what they do, so my job is to fill in the gaps in their presentation knowledge and to teach them the little things that they may not know—how to be powerful, relaxed, friendly, and *alive* in front of a group.

I think the most important gift that I offer my clients is this: I see their potential. I hold the vision of what is possible, I see the horizon—the strength, the command, the beauty, and elegance of their success. I see their *capacity*— not in the way that a clairvoyant sees the future, but more in the way that an architect envisions the curve of an entryway in a blueprint and in the way that a teacher sees the end result of a difficult learning process.

I provide the vision when it is most unclear and inaccessible to my clients. When it feels *impossible* to them, when they are flustered, nervous, overwhelmed, unmotivated, I show them what *is possible*. I hold the bar pretty high—I have a reputation for that! And what continues to astound me is that every single person exceeds it. That is the beauty of this work. I count my blessings every day that I am able to help people in this way—to hold this precious vision of their success right in front of them so they can see it too.

About the Author

Angela DeFinis is an author, speaker, trainer, and CEO/Founder of DeFinis Communications, Inc. She has spent over twenty years helping business professionals find solutions to their communication challenges and to develop a broader repertoire of potent speaking skills. Her pragmatic message and positive approach create personal and lasting change.

Founded in 1997, DeFinis Communications, Inc. offers a range of speaker services including executive and individual speaker coaching, corporate in-house programs, public seminars, media training, keynotes, and corporate events. Their popular *Encore! Elegant Skills for Powerful Presentations* program is a dynamic, hands-on learning laboratory where participants achieve results through high energy training activities, personalized attention, and compassionate coaching.

DeFinis Communications enjoys a reputation for results driven programs and services and exceptional customer partnerships. Valued clients include Autodesk, Avista Corp., Blue Shield of California, Charles Schwab, Coldwell Banker, Earthjustice, Hewlett Packard, Levi Strauss, Puget Sound Energy, Sendmail, Sun Microsystems, and Tyco.

Ms. DeFinis holds a Bachelor of Arts degree in English and a Master of Education degree in Counseling. She is a member of the American Society for Training and Development, the National Speakers Association, and the National Association of Women Business Owners.

Angela DeFinis

DeFinis Communications, Inc.

9 Altamira Avenue

Kentfield, CA 94904

Phone: 415.258.8176

adefinis@definiscommunications.com

www.definiscommunications.com

ROADMAP to SUCCESS 7

An interview with...

Michael Bruce

David Wright (Wright)

Today we're talking with Michael Bruce. Mr. Bruce is Founder and President of World of WOW, LLC, a premier provider of speaking, training, and coaching services committed to unleashing the most powerful potential of individuals. Mr. Bruce's track record of inspiring extraordinary results has made him one of the most sought-after keynote speakers in the field of human potential. With over two decades of hands-on experience, including Fortune 500, medium and small sized businesses, and entrepreneurial start-ups, Mr. Bruce has developed his expertise in accelerating the movement of individuals toward performing at their best. His creative blend of the best available knowledge, leading edge positions, and futurist foresight has proven extremely valuable to his clients. Mr. Bruce, nicknamed "That WOW Guy," is an idealist, dreamer, and visionary. He is a trusted advisor to many, a passionate pursuer of excellence in himself, and a believer in people's highest potential. Energetic, creative, inspiring, and driven, Mr. Bruce is a powerful catalyst for the changes that propel individuals and businesses to their greatness.

Michael, welcome to *Roadmap to Success*!

Michael Bruce (Bruce)

Thank you, David. I am delighted to be here.

Wright

Our purpose with *Roadmap to Success* is to share successful business strategies. Since individual performance is such a critical foundation for business success, it is only appropriate to devote Chapter One to you and The WOW Principle˝.

What is the key to having a successful business strategy?

Bruce

The single most determining factor in the sustainable success of any business is the alignment of inspired, energized, and fulfilled employees. I routinely advise businesses to spend more time and money developing people, not strategies. Even the best business strategies fail when individuals responsible for the execution underachieve—when individuals don't live up to their potential. Good business strategies fail because they can't compensate for underachievers. The opposite is true as well. Overachievers can often compensate for bad business strategies and the ever-changing demands of today's extremely competitive environment.

It's therefore critical that companies implement a process to develop individuals into overachievers, regardless of their current performance level, specific job responsibilities, or the overall business strategy. The WOW Principle provides the strategy, process, and critical success factors for individuals to unleash their powerful potential and be all they can be. This ultimately leads to a business that can remain competitive even under the most challenging situations.

Wright

It sounds as though you are suggesting that investing in the training and development of employees is the best business strategy.

Bruce

I'm not suggesting that this be the only business strategy, but it is the critical foundation if a company expects to execute any other strategy well. More importantly, it must be in place if a company wants to continuously differentiate itself from its competition and sustain a high level of performance over time.

Wright

So how would you suggest companies invest their training and development dollars?

Bruce

"Invest" is a great word to use. Unfortunately, the Return On Investment (ROI) of training dollars spent is often dramatically less than desired. The best way for companies to utilize their training dollars is to invest in a specialized program that coaches individuals to optimize their whole self. I strongly recommend a much more holistic approach to personal development than the typical training programs of today that focus on specific hard and soft skills. Businesses need to have a personal development program that includes topics related to self-discovery, self-discipline, self-esteem, emotional control, the psychology of achievement, and peak performance, as well as other success principles. This is how companies can help employees unleash their powerful potential and close the gap between their daily performance and their capabilities.

The WOW Principle addresses these topics. I like using a computer analogy. In this case, The WOW Principle helps to develop a highly functional, adaptable, flexible, and robust operating system within an individual. Standard hard and soft skill training is an attempt to load software onto this operating system. If the software isn't compatible with the individual's operating system, then it will not work. That training will not take hold within the individual. And even if the software runs on the operating system, wouldn't we want to optimize its effectiveness?

The WOW Principle strategies transform even the most unlikely individuals into overachievers who are then more determined and capable than ever to make a significant contribution at work. In most cases the shift in the individual's performance is immediate and dramatic. In some cases the transformation of the employee takes time and is more incremental. The bottom line is businesses don't have to feel they are gambling with their training budgets. The WOW Principle works and both individuals and businesses prosper.

Businesses need to help individuals build highly functional, adaptable, flexible, and robust operating systems in order for the hard and soft skills training to be most effective. With these robust operating systems, individuals become more capable of executing business strategies leading to a company's success.

Wright

Will you give us an example?

Bruce

Sure, let's take a generic communication skills class. The content of this training might include techniques on how to be an assertive communicator. Individuals can learn techniques to use but if they have low self-esteem and little confidence, then the training will never truly take hold. If we can help someone with strategies to improve their self-esteem and confidence, then the communication skills training will be much more effective and more likely to be embodied by the individuals.

In fact, if businesses work on an individual's operating system as I suggest, they won't have to spend as much time and money on soft skills. Let's look at listening skills for example—making eye contact, matching pace, asking probing questions, nodding affirmatively, and paraphrasing are techniques that might be covered in listening skills training. Businesses can choose to provide this kind of training or focus on helping individuals develop an unconditional positive regard and authentic curiosity in others. Which training will produce a better listener? Which training will be more effective helping individuals maintain good listening skills in pressure situations?

In the case of developing an unconditional positive regard and authentic curiosity in others, individuals would not have to consciously think about the listening techniques. Their subconscious mind will intuitively take over. Additionally, these individuals will perform better in team environments, dealing with difficult people, diffusing anger in the workplace, overcoming negativity, and resolving conflict and confrontation, just to name a few areas. Isn't it better to provide training that will help individuals excel across the wide array of social skills? Imagine the positive impact on an individual's life outside of the work environment.

Wright

I can see the tremendous benefit for businesses that invest in this type of program. The payoff could be great.

Bruce

I agree, especially in today's competitive business environment. Technology is bringing change to the marketplace at an ever-increasing rate. The Internet and transportation industries have contributed to the evolution of a world economy that operates twenty-four hours a day, three hundred and sixty-five days a year. There is an increase in the number of mergers, acquisitions, partnerships, and bankruptcies that are rewriting the landscape of various industries. In order for businesses to be successful in this highly fluid environment, they must rely on the creative collaboration of their people more than ever before. Businesses will have a competitive advantage if they build a culture that is focused on the self-improvement and personal growth of their employees.

Businesses must take a more proactive approach in developing each individual's operating system. This will help individuals build habits that lead to greater levels of happiness, success, and fulfillment throughout all areas of their lives. Businesses benefit through the improved performance that comes from these powerful strategies that energize employees. Employee satisfaction surveys show dramatic improvement. Turnover and related costs plummet when employees feel their company has an authentic interest in both their professional and personal growth. Tapping into the intrinsic motivators in each individual will ensure a captivated and committed team, ready to carry a business on their backs through the toughest of challenges. And we all know there will be challenges.

Wright

How did you become an authority in the field of human potential?

Bruce

My first conscious recognition of wanting to study human potential stemmed from a powerful lesson I learned back in 1984. It started on Induction Day at the United States Naval Academy. I was one of 1,100 freshmen (or "plebes" as we were called) fortunate enough to be selected from the over 20,000 applicants to begin a journey to become commissioned as an officer in the United States Navy. As freshman we were required to arrive two months earlier than the rest of the student body for Plebe Summer. This was my boot camp.

All the drill instructors seemed nice and helpful throughout that day. I remember getting a really cool new hairstyle and many new fashionable clothes. (Okay, the truth is I got my head completely shaved and was issued very uncomfortably stiff uniforms, but it was a very exciting day nevertheless.)

Everything was going smoothly until I put my hand down after taking the oath of office. The yelling started and I don't think it stopped all summer long. It was chaos!

I quickly found myself struggling. It didn't seem to matter how much studying I did, the platoon leaders would always find something I didn't know. Regardless of how much time I spent cleaning my room for inspection, they would use their bleached white gloves to attract dust from somewhere. When I thought my shoes were shined bright enough, they would tell me otherwise. No matter how fast I ran during physical training, it never seemed to be fast enough for them. The bottom line, regardless of my effort, the yelling and criticism didn't stop.

In order to survive I quickly adopted an attitude of ambivalence. I was able to rationalize not trying too hard or caring too much. It was my way of coping with the challenges and stress of the high pressure and chaotic environment.

The powerful lesson occurred when rankings came out at the end of the first half of the summer. In my squad of twelve, can you guess where I was ranked?

Wright

I don't want to be insulting but I'd have to say twelve?

Bruce

Fortunately yes.

Wright

You mean "unfortunately?"

Bruce

No. I really mean fortunately. This was the catalyst for me to travel down the road of studying human potential.

After telling me my ranking, my squad leader, John "Delly" Delcamp, saw the shock and shame on my face. I was struck by his ability to have an expression that conveyed not only empathy but high expectations as well. He leaned forward, put his hand on my shoulder, and in a very calm yet assertive voice said, "Michael, you are capable of so much more." Not giving me a chance to argue my case, he immediately dismissed me.

Initially I struggled with the ranking. How was this possible? Despite my ambivalence I had still clearly performed better than some of my squad mates. I was a wreck contemplating telling my mom and dad that I finished twelve of twelve in my squad. How disappointed they would feel after being so proud of me for my acceptance into the Naval Academy. I was stunned, but more importantly, painfully embarrassed.

As I shared the reality of my ranking with my parents, my dad did what he had done so well throughout my years growing up. Without making me feel guilty, and without disappointment in his voice, my dad just asked, "So what did you learn from this experience?" My dad is a great example of unconditional love and unwavering support.

The lesson I learned was powerful—the truest measure of our performance is relative to our own potential. We must not limit ourselves by comparisons to others, but rather dare ourselves to be all we can be. From this experience on, I was driven to discover the best ways to unleash my most powerful potential.

The words written by Marianne Williamson and spoken by Nelson Mandela during his 1994 inaugural speech resonate so powerfully on this point:

"Our deepest fear is not that we are inadequate.
Our deepest fear is that we are powerful beyond measure.
It is our light, not our darkness, that most frightens us.
We ask ourselves, who am I to be brilliant,
Gorgeous, talented, and fabulous?"

David, I'll ask you what John Delcamp asked me, "Are you capable of so much more?" How many of those listening or reading this interview feel as though they are living up to their potential? Everyone has a gap. I work with overachievers every day, and even the best of the best can't confidently say that they are being all they can be. This gap is where The WOW Principle thrives. I continuously challenge everyone to close their gap and The WOW Principle provides the pathway to help them achieve this.

It was this personal journey that began over twenty years ago that became my passion and ultimately the catalyst for me to try and lead other determined achievers to discover their greatness. The creation of the World of WOW is a direct result of my trying to live up to my potential by making a difference in the world.

Wright

It appears your Naval Academy experience was very instrumental in your journey. How else do you think your military service might have contributed to your success?

Bruce

Undoubtedly, the magnitude of my responsibility at such a young age accelerated my journey of self-discovery. I was pushed well beyond my comfort zone by the high-stakes assignments I was expected to accomplish. I participated in extremely sensitive military operations where any mistake could lead to aborting a critical mission and perhaps jeopardizing national security. I learned powerful lessons in accountability and how critical the elements of life-long learning and a strong work ethic are to performing at my best.

The list of benefits I received from beginning my career in the military is a long one. While many of my friends were still trying to figure out what they wanted to do after their playful college experience, I had the challenge of being the youngest department head on the waterfront, and was expected to perform at levels much beyond my years of experience. The powerful pull of high expectations was highlighted as an essential ingredient to bringing out the best in me. I certainly made mistakes along the way, but also learned greatly the benefit of natural consequences. I could go on and on.

Wright

Let's now turn our focus to The WOW Principle. Will you define WOW?

Bruce

WOW is POTENTIAL REALIZED™. It's the state when an individual feels powerful, confident, inspired, energized, and unstoppable. Like athletes being in "The Zone," being in a state of WOW feels effortless, yet produces astonishing results. Unfortunately many individuals don't operate at this level of performance too often, if ever at all. And it's even more rare to discuss this level of performance in the context of a work environment.

The idea of connecting WOW with human potential was born as I researched examples of amazing performances, great individual accomplishments, and the ability of people to overcome tremendous hardships. At times I just found myself saying "Wow!" I also began using this expression more and more in response to my own improved performance. WOW just became synonymous with my quest to understand the path to realizing potential.

Wright

You implied earlier that potential is relative to the individual. How do you answer those leaders who argue that some people will always underachieve and will never reach their potential?

Bruce

First, I wouldn't refer to anyone who made that argument as a true leader. The most successful leaders develop an unwavering belief in the capabilities of each and every individual. Secondly, I would explain to the critics that it is their own mental model that needs fixing. They are contributing greatly to the individual underachieving through a self-fulfilling prophecy model that is working in the wrong direction. This is an epidemic in society. We negatively impact others with our limiting beliefs and we are impacted negatively by others' limiting beliefs.

The best part about an individual's potential is that it is forever expanding and growing. It is a moving target. With more knowledge, experience, achievement, and accomplishments comes the greater potential and opportunity for success, happiness, and fulfillment.

Wright

So that brings to mind the question, can anyone ever truly reach his or her potential?

Bruce

I consider this a philosophical question more than anything else. I believe individuals can reach their potential but only for a split-second in time. Once someone performs at a given level, it's been accomplished and a new potential is created. The pursuit of reaching potential is really just a life-long journey in expanding potential. As an individual achieves, potential grows.

Realizing potential, or the pursuit of WOW as I refer to it, is a very personal journey. People must embrace change and learn to successfully navigate around their limiting beliefs, conditioned tendencies, and gremlins. There is a tremendous amount of self-awareness that is required to move toward manifesting one's greatness. At the end of each day it's important for each of us to look in the mirror and be both satisfied with our effort and honest with ourselves. Constructive self-criticism is essential to success.

Here's another great lesson I learned during the summer of '84. Drew Dryden Wannamaker was my roommate at the Naval Academy. Drew embodied the opposite of my ambivalence. He was an overachiever from day one. When I had enough of cleaning our room, Drew would continue. I would try to pressure Drew to stop, arguing that failure of our upcoming inspection was inevitable. It really didn't matter what I said. Drew would acknowledge my position, smile, and continue to clean. When I would go to sleep at lights out, Drew would stay up with a flashlight under his blanket studying more. I'm sure you get the picture.

Drew went on to finish in the top twenty of our class while earning a Systems Engineering degree, the toughest major offered at the Academy. He was selected to command a nuclear powered submarine by the age of thirty-six, and most recently fought and won his toughest battle ever—a battle with cancer.

At the end of the second half of the summer Drew was ranked last in his squad. We all knew why I had ranked last, but Drew routinely performed at a level far exceeding his peers. I remember attempting to console Drew, and he would have nothing of it. He explained to me that individuals are the best judges of their own performance. It is impossible to please everyone all the time, and it is this realization that can help free individuals in their journey to their own greatness. Ultimately we must answer to ourselves.

The ability of an individual to feel satisfied with his or her effort will help keep them on the self-development trail while the push of constructive self-criticism will help determine how far they can go.

Wright

That's a great point Drew made, and I can see its relevancy in a journey of self-discovery and personal growth.

Why don't we turn our attention to The WOW Principle?

Bruce

The WOW Principle has three major components: fundamental beliefs, critical development areas, and specific self-optimization techniques. It is the combination of all three components that helps an individual achieve optimum levels of happiness, success, and fulfillment. So, for those people who want to be all they can be, The WOW Principle provides the roadmap to get them there.

The fundamental beliefs component is made up of three specific laws that must be embodied if people expect to live up to their potential. It is the core foundation for creating more WOW. Individuals who don't embrace these laws bury their possibility for greatness.

Next, there are four development areas that require considerable attention and continued focus throughout an individual's self-development journey, and in his or her life, for that matter. These are the necessary ingredients required in the recipe of optimal performance.

And finally, The WOW Principle identifies powerful self-optimization and fulfillment techniques. These are the most effective tools that individuals can use to build an impenetrable life of happiness, success, and fulfillment. These proven strategies will help propel individuals down their personal development journeys faster and further then they ever imagined.

Wright

Will you take us through each of the three major components?

Bruce

We'll start with the three laws that make up the fundamental beliefs that those in pursuit of excellence must embody. They are the Laws of Possibility, Choice, and Authenticity.

The Law of Possibility states that the possibilities in any given situation are infinite. In this way, possibility becomes the fuel of potential. Too often individuals restrict themselves because they don't keep their minds open to what is possible. An individual's existence becomes like a car driving in first gear. They may be stepping on the gas pedal, and the engine may be revving and working hard, but they are extremely limited in how fast and far they can go. Without believing that individuals are capable of so much more, there will be little to no chance for them to move toward greater levels of success. If individuals can see it, and believe it, they can achieve it. Seeing it is about understanding the Law of Possibility.

Many people intellectually believe the Law of Possibility is true but they will argue that certain things aren't possible for them. The Law of Choice helps to address this argument. *The Law of Choice is essentially free will, and states that all people have the innate ability to choose their thoughts, feelings, and actions.* People must believe in self-determination to effectively travel down the road to top performance. Unfortunately, this is the most underutilized attribute of the human race. Too many individuals get into patterns of behavior and beliefs that lead to contentment and stagnation. Contentment is the enemy of Wow. Individuals must remain aggressive, adaptable, and agile. We live in a world of excuse-makers, blamers, and people who just refuse to be accountable for their circumstances. Simply put, individuals will never visit the WOWzone™ unless they embrace the core belief that they have the freedom to choose their path in all that they do.

I've dealt with many critics who argue that people can't change the way they feel, they only have the ability to choose how they respond. I disagree. Just as we have all developed conditioned tendencies throughout our lives, we can replace them with new ones. It just takes patience, practice, and persistence.

To round out the three fundamental beliefs is The Law of Authenticity. *The Law of Authenticity states that fulfillment in life is only possible if individuals are in harmony with themselves.* Some people refer to this as being true to yourself. So what does this mean? Too often people try to make themselves into something they are not. They believe that if they behave in a certain manner, obtain certain possessions, or have more money that they will become happier and more successful. The truth is that to be at their happiest and most fulfilled, individuals need to be aware of their uniqueness and take advantage of those areas. They need to avoid giving in to peer pressure or conforming to society norms. People need to march to the beat of their own drum. It is each individual's uniqueness that must be harnessed to achieve his or her greatness. People spend too much time trying to be like others, who sadly, most often aren't even happy with themselves.

Wright

I can see how these three fundamental beliefs are critical to people's ability to reach their potential.

Let's move on to the four development areas. Please tell us about these.

Bruce

The development areas within The WOW Principle direct people to the four key fields of study where individuals must build extreme competence if they expect to ever live up to their individual potential. The four development areas are Passions, Purpose, Self-Awareness, and Goal Management.

We begin any intervention with a client by assessing where that individual currently resides within these development areas. We then take a linear approach to building competencies in each area. Eventually we expect individuals to be working in parallel on all four areas, but during the initial learning phase of The WOW Principle, the linear approach has proven most effective. Initially, the strength of each development area will depend on competence in the previous one.

In the development area of Passions we use exercises and powerful questions to help individuals reconnect with their intrinsic motivators. We want to find out what values and activities energize them. Having a complete grasp of these passions will help people find the gaps between their current existence and where they must travel if they expect to ever reach their potential.

Too often we find that individuals have suppressed those very values and activities that bring the most joy and happiness to them. We all had dreams when we were growing up. We wanted to be astronauts and doctors, firemen and teachers. What happened to these visions that brought us so much excitement and passion? We want people to explore the same unlimited potential they felt when they were children and were filled with unrestrained dreams. The WOW Principle is about turning dreams and fantasies into reality.

We next study an individual's purpose for living. You may be surprised, but most people cannot identify their purpose in life. Our goal is to align the previously identified passions with a powerful purpose—a deep-seated declaration that provides the overall direction of their journey toward fulfillment. Our legacy exercise asks individuals to imagine their funeral and what they would want people to be saying about them. We want each individual to gain clarity on the meaning of his or her individual life. Without great purpose, individuals will fall short of reaching their best.

Once individuals have a better understanding of their passions and purpose we challenge them to investigate what is limiting their achievement and personal growth. It is an individual's mental model that unconsciously limits their potential. We work with individuals to develop tremendous self-awareness. We help them identify the limiting beliefs and blind spots that hold them back. The use of assessment tools in studying an individual's communication, behavior, and leadership styles might be examined. We study conflict resolution preferences and learning styles. We perform 360-degree evaluations to help individuals gain clarity of the perception others have of them. Everything we can do to build greater self-awareness helps an individual become more happy, successful, and fulfilled. Ultimately, greater self-awareness helps people more effectively navigate the challenges and obstacles they will inevitably face on their journey. We used a variety of Emotional Intelligence and Social Intelligence theory in this development area.

Eventually we find our way to Goal Management. With the three other development areas blossoming, our clients are now ready to create a plan that will pull them toward their greatness. Initially, most people say they have goals, but upon further scrutiny, their planning and goal setting fall significantly short of being effective. Most people have been introduced to effective goal management strategies, but for some reason choose not to implement them. When we hold our clients accountable for effective goal management, this dramatically accelerates their journey toward greater levels of happiness, success, and fulfillment.

Wright

I get the impression that The WOW Principle isn't for the faint of heart. You challenge individuals to explore deep-rooted beliefs and habits that may be hindering their success.

Bruce

I can't agree more. The WOW Principle provides a very broad and comprehensive approach to helping an individual realize his or her potential, but the person must be open to change—significant change. I only work with clients who truly convince me of their commitment to this lifestyle.

Wright

Let's cover the final component of The WOW Principle—self-optimization and fulfillment techniques.

Bruce

There are many powerful tools and proven strategies that can help individuals in all phases of performance. Most individuals want to find more time in the day, be better communicators, more organized, less stressed, healthier, and more effective. The list goes on and on.

We work with individuals and companies to identify these performance improvement possibilities. Our techniques run the gamut from using visualization and affirmations to specific methodology for managing e-mails and workflow. The tools introduced first will vary for each individual and are dependent upon what transpires during his or her development area examination. We really have put together the best-of-the-best toolbox of self-optimization strategies for people to choose from. Not every tool works for every individual, but we have such an overwhelming collection of proven methods that every individual will find transformation possible.

Wright

You mentioned the areas of Emotional and Social Intelligence earlier. What other areas of influence and personal experiences have helped you develop The WOW Principle?

Bruce

In my years after the Navy I spent some time in medical product sales before going to work for a struggling biotech company and then a highly successful telecommunications company. My experiential learning was invaluable during these years. It was as though I had a lab of employees to play with as I worked with individuals to develop practices that worked. My ideas were tested time and time again with real life employees in real life pressure situations and my learning continued.

It was clear to me during my early academic studies in personality theory and social psychology that most individuals underachieve dramatically. I remember the motivational training of Stephen Covey and Anthony Robbins being very instrumental in my personal and professional development. And it was the leadership training of Ken Blanchard that also aided in my career success. Undoubtedly, all three men have in some way contributed to the backbone that has become The WOW Principle. Others such as Brian Tracy, Dr. Tony Alessandra, Zig Ziglar, David Rock, and Wayne Dyer are a piece of The WOW Principle puzzle as well. All of these mentors touch on common themes and elements that can help individuals achieve greater levels of happiness, success, and fulfillment.

More recently the strength-based movement that Marcus Buckingham has made so popular and the developments in Positive Psychology from Martin Seligman had an impact on me, as well.

The Strozzi Institute, www.strozziinstitute.com, just north of San Francisco, in Peteluma, California, is doing phenomenal work helping people unleash their most powerful potential. They provide a gift that I can only describe as an ability to take action that previously seemed impossible. More importantly Strozzi programs help individuals embody the learning that leads to sustainable action. If businesses and individuals could invest in only one personal development program, I would send them to Strozzi. In all my research I have not found more effective and powerful programs than those Dr. Richard Strozzi-Heckler has developed. There are many popular brands in the self-help industry but none have more proven substance and impact than Strozzi programs. Take a look.

It seemed that over the years I would find pieces of the self-development puzzle, but there wasn't one place where I could go to understand all the fundamental beliefs, critical development areas, and self-optimization techniques. That's where The WOW Principle was born. It was my effort to consolidate the best of the best from all the greatest minds I had studied in the human potential dimension.

Wright

Well, you are certainly making an impact today! I'm sure our listeners and readers are interested in how you came to transition from senior management in corporate America to your current success in the public spotlight.

Bruce

The truth is that most of my effort and education was geared toward my own self-improvement and personal development. I was attempting to live the best life possible for me. I was walking down a very personal trail of growth and exploration when I attended the La Jolla's Writers Conference in 2005. I was sitting at lunch speaking with some other attendees and having a very stimulating conversation about the writing industry. There was a lady at our table who had a very powerful presence. She exuded clarity, confidence, and compassion. It wasn't necessarily the words that she spoke, but the way in which she presented herself that impressed me. Her implicit communication was so powerful.

As she left the table I inquired into the background of this wonderful lady. Her name was Catherine Ryan Hyde and she is author of *Pay it Forward*. The major motion picture, *Pay it Forward,* starring Kevin Spacey and Helen Hunt, was based on her book. The movie was released and distributed by Warner Brothers in 2000. A real-life social movement emerged based upon her theme of spreading kindness to strangers. These heartfelt acts would influence others to do the same. Paying it forward became infectious.

I had a few more interactions with Catherine throughout the conference as she inquired about my purpose for attending. At the very end of the conference Catherine made a point to come over to me and give me her business card, which she was very selective about handing out. As she said goodbye she added one more thing, "You have something special to say, Michael—*you* should pay it forward!" Her challenge was the catalyst I needed to jump from the safety and security of corporate America to form World of Wow, LLC and focus on helping others reach their potential. Part of my purpose became spreading my knowledge and trying to help other determined achievers in pursuit of their own greatness.

Catherine was the inspiration behind WOWcards¨, a simple tool available free on my Website that helps people pay it forward. I challenge all those who hear me speak to visit my Web site and start using WOW cards. Recognizing the efforts and contributions of others helps many individuals escape from their jail of negativity. Use of this tool helps retrain their subconscious toward having a more positive disposition and thought pattern, which ultimately better positions them for their own success.

I also created the Hall of WOW ¨ as a collection of true stories that exemplify The WOW Principle in action. In the near future I plan to publish these inspiring stories to recognize those individuals who have made such a powerful difference in people's lives. I encourage everyone to nominate an influential person in his or her life. Nominees receive a Certificate of

Induction into the WOW Hall of Fame and have the possibility of getting their stories published.

Wright

I encourage our audience today as well as those who may read this in the future to take full advantage of your offerings. What else is on the horizon for Michael Bruce and the World of WOW?

Bruce

Much more of the same, I hope. I will continue my focus and efforts to lead others toward their greatness. Though I've been involved on a personal level in the field of human potential for over two decades, I am at the early stages of being in the public spotlight. I'd love for leaders at every level in organizations to call and discuss the best way we can make a substantive positive impact within their organizations.

My passion truly lies in speaking face-to-face with both large and small audiences as well as teams that are in search of significantly better results. I want to fill my calendar with more speaking engagements and training workshops both domestically and internationally. My travels have been extensive, but I know many are still unaware of The WOW Principle and the powerful potential they each possess.

I'm a certified Evidenced Based Coach and credentialed by the International Coaches Federation. Though I'm always interviewing prospective clients, I only partner with individuals who demonstrate a true commitment to self-discovery and personal development. By limiting my active client list, I'm able to provide an extremely high degree of focus, commitment, and service. I enjoy coaching work teams as well. It's amazing what is possible when a group of individuals truly commits to becoming a team. There is no greater honor and privilege than to share in breakthrough moments with my clients.

I'll continue my efforts as an author. *WOWisms*™ will be published in 2008 and is a compilation of inspiring quotes with powerful coaching questions and journaling space to help individuals identify key themes in their lives. I'm also working on *From Ow to Wow*™: *Thriving Through Change* for release in early 2009.

I'll also continue my search for the best time management techniques so I can find the time to do it all!

Wright

Well, what a great conversation. Today we have been talking with Michael Bruce who is Founder and President of World of Wow, LLC, a company dedicated to leading individuals and businesses to unleash their most powerful potential. I just have one more thing to say, "Wow!"

Bruce

Thanks so much, David.

ABOUT THE AUTHOR

Michael Bruce, nicknamed "That WOW Guy," is an idealist, dreamer, and visionary. Energetic, creative, inspiring, and driven, Michael is a powerful catalyst for changes that propel individuals and businesses to their greatness.

For over twenty-two years, Michael has studied the art and science of human potential, success, and fulfillment. His education includes a diverse foundation in theories of leadership and management, coaching and psychology, personality theory, communication, adult development, organizational systems, social psychology, humanistic psychology, positive psychology, cognitive behavioral techniques, and emotional and social intelligence theory.

First as decorated naval officer and then in senior management positions within the biotech and telecommunications industries, Michael has come to understand what it takes to excel in highly stressful, continuously changing, and extremely competitive environments. His corporate and entrepreneurial experience, along with an MBA in Technology Management, provide Michael with amazing insight into how the powerful potential of individuals can be harnessed to achieve sustainable business success.

A Naval Academy Athletic Hall of Fame Inductee and named an Outstanding Young Man in America in 1988, Michael is currently an active member of the National Speakers Association, a credentialed coach by the International Coaches Federation, certified trainer by the American Society of Training and Development, a committed life-long learner, and pursuer of excellence.

Michael Bruce
World of WOW, LLC
9921 Carmel Mountain Road
#WOW
San Diego, CA 92129-2813

888.WOW.8WOW
Fax: 888.216.3318
michael.bruce@theworldofwow.com
www.theworldofwow.com

ROADMAP to SUCCESS 8

An interview with...

Natalie R. Manor, CEO

David Wright (Wright)

Today we're talking with Natalie Manor who is the CEO of Natalie Manor & Associates (NMA), The Roadmap. For the past twenty-two years Natalie has been privileged to work with leaders and professionals who want to create success in their professional and personal lives. As she has coached and consulted with these highly motivated business leaders, she's asked them what has created value for them in the work that they do together. A universal answer is that they gain awareness of what is most important in their lives and in the lives of the people around them. With this awareness they have the ability to improve their performance and create success, they know what is needed and valued, then they can communicate clearly with impact and without the mystery. To that end, these clients' experiences have inspired her to develop the "Roadmap to Creating High Value Relationships," CHVR_{SM} program and The Roadmap Series of programs and products.

Natalie, welcome to *Roadmap to Success.*

Natalie Manor (Manor)

Thank you so much. I'm delighted to be invited to contribute my experience and valuable programs for all of you who are interested in producing your own roadmap to ultimate success.

Wright

Well, thank you. What in your work guided you to know that creating high valuable relationships (CHVR) was a valuable and needed concept?

Manor

We at NMA have been working in leadership and executive development for twenty-two years helping business professionals understand the importance of communication in producing effectiveness and successful results. What we continued to uncover was that even the best and most competent leaders were exhibiting difficulty with executing their goals because of communication inefficiencies. In our experience, it does not matter if the organization was entrepreneurial or a large global corporation, communication clarity was difficult to achieve. Since the communication process was difficult and unclear, the organizational relationships—whether employee-to-employee—dealing with prospective clients, supplying customers, or developing vendor relationships, were many times unproductive and unsuccessful.

How do we really communicate well? What is interesting about communicating well? It is really a very basic concept. We know that it is not only a valuable concept, but also ultimately connects professional success and business profits. We call it CHVR, Creating High Value Relationships. When creating a high value relationship, the core is communication. People want to be influential and productive when they communicate. When they aren't, the two foundational aspects that are missing are the awareness of how to communicate well and the perceived lack of time to communicate well. People say they have run out of time to communicate well, but communicating well is at the core of creating a high value relationship with people.

We developed CHVR for those business professionals who felt like they did not have time to communicate well. They were not creating high value relationships within their organizations, with their staff, within their teams, with their stakeholders, with their stockholders, even within their own families. They were moving so fast that they had forgotten that the relationship was really most important and the glue was effective communication.

Wright

So who are the people who benefit the most from developing awareness and understanding around creating high value relationships and effective communication?

Manor

In my experience, once people understand what creating a high value relationship is they realize they already know how to do it well with many people. An example: I would assume that you have relationships that are just perfect for you—a college roommate, a partner/spouse, family, a great friend—people with whom you find it easy to communicate and spend time. Those are already high value relationships for you. However, there are those with whom you have a very difficult time communicating—the two of you just do not connect. The chemistry between the two of you is difficult. There is very little ease in communicating or even being around each other. The answer to your question is: *all* people benefit from knowing how to create a high value relationship, especially when it is difficult. There will always be those people with whom you have difficulty communicating. These individuals may include your boss, the new board of director's member, or the hot new client, and you must communicate effectively with them.

We teach people to replicate what they already know how to do instinctively with those they communicate with easily and successfully. They learn to use these relationships as examples of how to communicate effectively in difficult but necessary relationships. We teach them to replicate what they already know how to do almost instinctively because successful communicators want to create influence, clarity, results, profits, guaranteed sustainability, and impact with all people.

Our training program works for people who are leaders, managers, or anyone who really needs to replicate what they already know and do brilliantly, with their own high value relationships. Through CHVR anyone can learn how to create a high value relationship with people they don't already know and/or they may not have that relationship with. We give them the roadmap to learn how to easily create influential and high impact communication with those people.

Wright

So why is influential communication and knowing the "Seven Principles of CHVR" key to someone's successful performance?

Manor

Let me share with you a bit of information before I answer your terrific question. *Harvard Business Review* annually provides data regarding the needed and sought-after skills in leadership success. Wharton Business School is another source of data regarding the success of leadership within organizations. *Harvard Business Review* has reported that when organizations, small or large, global or local, look for leaders to run their organizations, they are looking for leaders who have the component of 85 percent interpersonal skills with 15 percent technical skills.

The CHVR Seven Principles reside in the interpersonal skill area—they are the key principals in creating influential and high impact communication. The Seven Principles of creating high value relationships are also where the ability to create an organization and/or a community that knows what it needs to do in order to do what is required for profits, favorable outcomes, goal achievement, and organizational development. Communication drives the success and results of the organization because with successful communication everyone understands what they need to do in order to be successful.

The Hawthorne Study that was done first in 1927, was the first psychological study that highlighted the need to provide clarity in communication and feedback to people for their contribution. Now most of us want to have positive feedback, but no feedback is worse than negative feedback. If people never get feedback on how they are doing or what their contribution is, it can create derision within the relationship or organization. The Hawthorne study was our first steppingstone to understanding what humans need. They need feedback, positive or negative. And in needing feedback they need clear communication. When a team, organization, family, or individual begins to understand the power of their communication with others, they understand how to create successful outcomes and results.

My point in referencing the *Harvard Business Review*, Wharton School of Business, and the Hawthorne Study is to emphasize the long-term and continued importance given to the act of communicating with clarity and influence.

Wright

Well I can't wait to hear what the Seven CHVR Principles are. Will you share them with our readers?

Manor

Of course. Here they are. The Seven Principles for Creating High Value Relationships are:

- Rapport,
- Context setting,
- Words versus meaning,
- Matching and Mirroring,
- Removing Preoccupation/ Judgment
- Curiosity and,
- Creating Clarity/ What Is Most Important (WIMI).

Most of our work has been done at the executive level, and includes managers and entrepreneurs. We have not run into any success-seeking individual who was able to communicate well, significantly, and consistently without demonstrating the skills of the Seven Principles of Creating High Value Relationships. Although there have been different variations, each principle continues to be significant to creating lasting success in the communication process.

The first principle for creating high value relationships is *rapport*. When information is clear, when the chemistry is there, and you can feel a sense of trust, you have rapport. It feels as though you can create whatever is important to the situation. With rapport there is an ease to the situation and the ability to move forward in your communication. Once you understand rapport you will also be able to recognize easily when you are out of rapport.

The second principle is *context setting*. This is important because we deal with so much information every moment. Whether we deal with people or issues, in person on the phone or in writing, we need to make sure that we know what we are communicating about. Our high school teachers wanted all of us to learn the what, where, how, when, and why of communication. It is the same with setting context. Don't assume that what is being discussed or negotiated is clear. Say what it is and continue to repeat the information until you are sure people are clear. The perfect way to see if there is agreement and understanding is to ask.

I'll give you an example of where context setting or the lack thereof can create significant communication issues. A huge potential problem-maker for each of us is e-mail. How many do we write each day? How many do we receive each day? Also, e-mail has become the preeminent way that all of us consistently use to communicate with each other. Here are a few ways you can avoid the pitfalls of communicating by e-mail. Make sure that when communicating you:

· Change subject lines to match the topic of the current e-mail message

· Restate what the topic is

· Exclude those who do not need to be included on the communication

Once a decision/conclusion is reached, restate it in the message. For example: "Yes, Tuesday at 1:00 PM is good for me to meet you at the Chinese restaurant Bok Cho on Spruce Street."

Our e-mail communication is sometimes a multiple series of ideas and notes, so resetting the context saves time and helps you know what it is you are discussing and when.

Resetting the context is an excellent idea in all communication whether in person or not. Ending a meeting/discussion with restating the decisions and next steps is critical to all those involved. Setting context creates clarity and eliminates errors.

The next principle is *words versus meanings*. In the seminars that we do for organizations and associations, each area of the world has certain words and certain meanings that are very different and do not mean the same thing. In the United Kingdom, they put things in their "boot," which is the trunk of their car. In the United States, it would be very odd to say "let's put it in the boot." When you go to New Jersey and you want a submarine sandwich, you ask for a hoagie. When I moved from Virginia to New England I asked for a milkshake and got a watery, milky drink, not the thick, ice cream-filled delight I anticipated. In New England a milkshake is a Frappe. These examples create lots of fun during the seminars and team meetings, and they also bring out a significant issue: Do people understand what we are saying? Do they understand what you mean?

If you have a word or phrase that is understood differently in different geographical areas, then you could really create inaccuracies in your schematics. If you are creating the next shield for NASA, you could cause a dangerous situation. You could really be in trouble if you're an engineer executing a drawing or you're a salesperson filling out an order or you're marketing doing the layout for the international trade show. We have become a global society so understanding what is really meant is truly important to creating successful outcomes.

The fourth CHVR principle is *matching and mirroring*. In-person communication, whether one-on-one or in meetings, holds the promise of being able to be in rapport with people by mirroring and matching their body language. The intentional behavior helps create clarity and ease in communication. Here is an example: Imagine someone sitting with you right now and she is sitting back in a chair, looking at the ceiling, and playing with a pen. What would this body language indicate to you? Would you get the indication from the person's body language that he or she was totally disinterested in you? I would. Body language is 55 percent of how we communicate and it speaks volumes about whether we are in rapport.

Another example: Imagine that you are at your favorite hotel and you've just entered your room. The bed is not made and the bathroom has not been cleaned. You are tired and you didn't get any dinner and the plane came in late. All you want to do is relax and read your newspaper. Now you are marching down the hallway toward the clerk at the front desk. With intensity, you want to make sure that this clerk understands that you are *not* happy, you can't believe the room is not ready, you are tired, and so on. You express to this clerk that you are upset. Meekly the clerk on the other side of the desk says softly, "I'm really sorry sir/ma'am." What happens next is the perfect example of mirroring and matching to create rapport and clarity.

Because the response from the clerk was soft and submissive, it did not match your intensity. Now you now raise your voice to the clerk. *"I don't think you understand my issue here!"* If the clerk was really clear about how to create immediate rapport with you about the room situation, he or she would stand and match your voice tone and speed of speaking. They would mirror and match your body language and intensity. You know what would happen? You would immediately feel listened to and understood. If the clerk really wanted to make you feel good, he or she would stomp down the hall with you and look at the condition of the room. That clerk would become your best friend at that moment because you would know he or she understood the importance of your issue and request. Mirroring and matching body language and intensity creates rapport.

Many people have expressed that this might create confrontation. However, when someone mirrors and matches our body language, we actually feel heard and understood. When we feel heard and understood, trust and respect is created.

The next principle is removing *preoccupation and judgment*. We are all so busy. We have endless lists things to do. Because of our many commitments and obligations we attend meetings, send/receive e-mail, and communicate while completely preoccupied. We are preoccupied with what we need to do next, we're preoccupied with what the person is wearing, we're preoccupied with the fact that the last time you dealt with this lady or gentleman, he or she didn't supply the report you wanted, or you don't like the way the person keep his or her office. You're sitting there completely preoccupied and in judgment. I could say you're probably not communicating very well are you? If you are preoccupied, you are not listening. The other person you are communicating with can feel that something is not working as well as it could. People can see it in your body language or hear it in your voice. By the way, if you are preoccupied with other thoughts, so are they. In my humble opinion, preoccupation cannot ever be totally erased; however, rapport and excellence in communication can be improved by knowing you are preoccupied. A deep breath before any conversation, e-mail, or meeting allows you to get in touch with what is important so you can create clarity during your communication. Preoccupation keeps us from listening, understanding, and creating clarity. Our next principle also helps with the issue of preoccupation.

Our sixth principle: *getting curious.* One of the best ways to eliminate preoccupation and judgment is to become curious. When you demonstrate curiosity, you look and sound like you are interested. The body tends to lean toward the speaker, questions are asked rather than just opinions being given, and the energy of the communication is high with expectation. Curiosity is a key tool in your communication toolbox, especially if someone has insulted you or your ego kicks in.

For example, if somebody says to you, "You know what, you haven't done this right in the last six months, and I'm not sure you're ever going to do it right." In most situations, you would probably feel a bit put off by the comment—maybe you'd even be angry. However, if you get curious, your mind cannot be angry or offended. You can't express these two emotions at the same time. Curiosity gives you time to adjust and it gives you the setting to create rapport in a difficult moment. It takes away all of the negativity because you can't be angry and you can't be ego-centered if you're curious. It works every time.

The seventh and final principle for creating high value relationships is *creating clarity/WIMI.* WIMI stands for What Is Most Important. We have found that asking, "What is most important to you?" is the single most effective question for creating clarity. That means asking people what they mean and what is most important to them.

You might ask: "So I'm hearing from you that this is important to you. Do I understand you correctly?" Or, "In this meeting what would be most important to you that we complete, that we find out, that we pay, that we receive, that we produce?"

Do you know that the majority of the people we have coached with, consulted with, and trained with have never been asked what would be *most* important to them? When you create clarity with people you are in rapport, you're curious, you are not preoccupied, you are mirroring and matching, you understand the meaning of the words that they're using, you've set the context in a way that they can understand, and you can produce all the results and successes that you want. Humans want and need that kind of attention and clarity. They need rapport. Once you master these principles, your communication will create remarkable and consistent results.

Wright

Are there one or two principles that are more important than the others in creating successful relationships and profound communication?

Manor

The first principle is *curiosity*. The business professionals and leaders I coach and train have found that getting curious is most effective in removing the emotion from any difficult situation. I also believe that when you're beginning to really practice creating influential communication through the Seven Principles, setting context and creating clarity with WIMI (What Is Most Important) produce rapport without fail.

I wanted to comment additionally about the principles we put together and why they're valuable. I believe that the reason rapport is so important is that it creates trust and respect. When you are in rapport with someone you trust, the person respects you and your information immediately. As you participate in context setting, you're creating clarity so you can have successful results. As you mirror and match body language to create rapport, you present to that other person, to that group, to that organization, that they are being listened to. When people feel like they're listened to, there's profoundness about the interaction. They feel valued.

When you become aware of your preoccupations and your judgment, you can easily remove any blocks for people being able to communicate with you. Both learning and performance are increased by removing preoccupation and judgment. When you get curious, you're ego is diminished and you're able to be open to your creativity in the moment. When you understand the words versus their meanings, you understand what is being said. When you create clarity through WIMI you find out what is really most important to that other person. You complete the cycle of communication and bring yourselves into rapport.

Wright

Would you have a case study or an example of how one or more of these communication principles have created impact and improved performance?

Manor

I have hundreds of examples of business professionals successfully learning and using CHVR to create influential communication and I'll share with you two of my favorites. I think these examples are some of the best ways of really understanding how the Seven Principals for Creating a High Value Relationship really work.

I worked with a CEO of a major manufacturing firm in New England. I was invited in to work with him on his speaking skills. One of the first things I do whenever I work with anyone, whether it's a team, an individual, or an organization, is an assessment. We complete an assessment so we can plot their roadmap for success outcomes. The assessment is a snapshot of where they are presently concerning skills and execution. From the assessment we design a roadmap for success and develop outcomes that are the desired results we want to create and sustain.

During my initial conversation with this CEO, I asked him, "What is really most important to you about our potentially working together?" He said he had a capital campaign that he wanted to put together for the foundation he worked with. Because he would be speaking at many functions to help raise awareness and dollars, he did not feel as articulate as he thought he should. He wanted me to help him put together a series of speeches he could use for the capital campaign.

We took a look at his current communication practices and found several that could be improved—body language, setting context, creating clarity with outcomes, and creating trust through rapport. His initial communication skills did not have adequate impact and were not as influential as they could be. We worked on building his confidence. During our work together, it came to light that he was a wonderful storyteller. We created five to six signature stories that came from his experiences that he could relate with confidence and passion.

Not only did the roadmap we designed for him to create influence and impact work in his presentations from the lectern, but his communication skills improved with is executive team, his board of directors, and his community. As I share this information with you, I can still remember his signature stories. He was able to produce memorable and influential communication with them. We worked together for more than two years. As he grew as a competent communicator, he decided to participate in the local community theater (singing and dancing). Not surprisingly, the foundation raised more money than it had ever raised before. He was also honored as Leader of the Year.

What made the difference was he understood the value of influential communication and that it wasn't just the words he was used—he was using his whole body to communicate. He came to truly understand that creating rapport with different people required him to practice the Seven Principles CHVR in his communication. He needed to create a high value relationship instantaneously with each one of those people, not only the donors, but also the community, and his organization. He became influential, but he wasn't communicating using just the speeches he delivered. The community felt communicated with in a way that allowed them to support the outcomes that he presented. People started writing big checks.

My other example is very, very exciting. I am working with a small technology company that is growing rapidly. Their internal issues have kept them from clearly communicating. They can fix anything and their clients are loyal. However, their internal communication needed an overhaul. After we completed all the assessments, these very smart people saw easily where creating a high value relationship internally was a key to their growth. We put into place a series of meetings practicing the Seven Principles, which has lead to a new understanding among the staff and the managers.

When you deal with a small technology company like this one—people who are committed to excellence and success—the learning curve is less steep. They have produced results that even they are surprised with. Because of their communication and the Seven Principles for success, they are in the process of buying and merging with a terrific little company that will add tremendous benefits to their already stellar offerings of service and sales.

Here is an example of their progress. The newly promoted VP told me that because they had learned how to be in rapport in the most difficult situations, a controversial and confrontational situation was totally avoided on a key issue. He said, "two months ago I would have told you 'this is hogwash'—being aware and creating rapport was a waste of my time." Then he said, "You know what Natalie, I'm really annoyed at you." When I asked why, he said, "Because there was an article and interview in our industry magazine with Jack Welch. . . he said exactly what you had been saying for the last six months."

"Hey, I like hanging out with Jack Welch," I said, "and I like being compared with him."

These are just two examples of the success of learning influential communication through the Seven Principles of CHVR. There are so many other stories about people who have produced successful and sustainable results using these principles that produce excellence in communication. Once you provide the roadmap for producing these kinds of results, very smart people and organizations that are seeking success begin learning and using the principles.

Wright

So, what is the one challenge of influential communication and CHRV that is the toughest to use or learn?

Manor

The most misused, avoided, hiding in the closet, shaking in their boots, challenge is delivering *difficult information successfully* while creating clarity and removing your preoccupations. When I can show people that delivering difficult information is not about confrontation, but improving someone's performance, either individually, as a team, or the organization, they want to begin practicing the new skill that very moment. I get to deal with really bright people and smart people who want to create really successful results.

We have a several formats—teleclasses, MP3s, CDs, seminars, trainings—in our roadmap series for delivering difficult information successfully. It is one of our most popular topics because people are reluctant to deliver difficult information for many reasons. Once they understand that they can deliver difficult information successfully— firings, performance plans, bad news, layoffs, lack of profits—and create increased performance and productivity, they want to learn how immediately.

Wright

So why do these principles create success, impact, and performance improvement?

Manor

You know, it's really simple: it helps people feel confident about themselves and their communication. People feel good when they're listened to and they feel respected. When you create rapport in a situation, people feel listened to and they feel respected. They trust the source of the information, they want to participate, and they want to contribute to the success of the outcomes.

When people feel confident about their communication skills they feel good. Their performance is better, their productivity is high, they are excited about coming to work, and they trust you, even if you're going to give them information that may not be to their liking.

Wright

So what do you want your readers to get from the work and the information you have provided her—what is the most important thing for them to learn and practice?

Manor

I want people to know that there is a roadmap—a guide—for them to guarantee their success. I want them to know that people are highly predictable in a unique way. I want our readers to understand that in creating their roadmap to success they will find out what is most important to themselves and to those around them. They will want to replicate the Seven Principles for CHVR because they were developed based on tried and true experiences by highly effective and successful people. I want them to see how quickly and easily they will create their own success- how rewarding it is to communicate well. Some great questions to ask themselves are:

Who am I as a leader?

Who am I as a communicator?

Who am I as a contributor?

Who am I as a leader?

Most of the majority of our successful leaders and communicators were not born that way; they worked hard on their skills to hone them in a way that served what is most important to them, their outcomes and goals, and what they want in their lives. Because we are all so amazingly busy, we can easily lose our way. CHVR is a roadmap that will always help you get back on track. We can provide many ways for you to design and discover your roadmap to successful outcomes.

Practice what you value. Learn what you don't know by asking. Do what is uncomfortable and maybe hard and then ask someone you respect how you are doing. Excellence in communication will always serve you well. Knowing how to communicate well will never be something you will regret learning. Creating rapport and trust with other highly motivated and successful individuals will only add to how interesting and successful your life can be. When you figure out who you are and who they are, you can have whatever you want, whenever you want it.

Wright

You know a wise man told me one time, many, many years ago that if I were walking down the road and saw a turtle sitting on the top of a fencepost, I could bet that he didn't get up there by himself. So would you tell our readers who have been your mentors throughout your twenty-two years of business?

Manor

I've had so many brilliant mentors. Ken Blanchard and Stephen Covey are two of my mentors. Their principles for business and personal success are solid and replicated by highly successful individuals and organizations throughout the world.

Another one of my mentors is Jack Welch. He is no-nonsense and very clear about what produces success.

Wayne Dyer, a metaphysical writer, really speaks to me. I have grown in my self-improvement and confidence by studying his teachings. Then there are countless businesswomen you've probably never heard of, but they continue to be key in my learning and development. I was in human resources and sales/marketing before I opened my consultancy and developed my own business. There were many I reached out to who helped me develop my success roadmap and inspired me to found "Your Roadmap to Extraordinary Success" programs and products.

Last but not least is Barbara Walters. She inspired me in a way that no else could. She was the first woman as a national TV anchor to make a salary of one million dollars—she broke the million dollar level for women. People were angry at her and she received hate mail because of her achievement. I sent her a personal handwritten note telling her how proud I was of her achievement and her talent. She actually sent me back a personal note and said that my words and best wishes meant a great deal to her. She opened a door for me that allowed me to step it up, move on out, and practice these classic success principles for myself and my clients.

Wright

Natalie, I've really learned a lot from your work and content. I know our readers have also. Your enthusiasm and commitment to this work is impressive.

Manor

Thanks so much. Life is good! I am delighted to share what I have learned and what my clients have achieved. A roadmap for success is just waiting for people to reach out and do what it takes to create it. I am happy to help people create their roadmaps and help them make their goals and dreams a reality.

Wright

Natalie Manor is Founder and CEO of Natalie Manor & Associates. She was educated in Psychology and Education at Ohio University and has advanced training from Georgetown University, James Madison University, University of Lowell, and the University of New Hampshire. She is a member of the National Speakers Association (NSA), the International Coaching Federation (ICF), and is certified by the American Society for Training and

Development (ASTD). She holds the distinction of being certified by the Executive Coaching Institute as an executive coach.

Natalie, thank you so much for contributing your business success ideas to *Roadmap to Success*.

Manor

My pleasure. Thanks for asking such terrific questions so our readers can begin to discern for themselves what is possible in developing their own roadmap to extraordinary success.

ABOUT THE AUTHOR

Natalie R. Manor, founder of the Roadmap to Your Extraordinary Success and CEO of Natalie Manor & Associates, is a remarkable individual and businesswoman. With more than twenty-two years of communication experience working with highly successful clients, Manor has produced a doable roadmap for all success minded individuals who want create a powerfully successful life.

Manor has coauthored four additional books on leadership, success, communication and stress. The *Roadmap* series includes 10 CDs/mp3s with action guides and activity sheets developed for individuals, teams and organizations. This compelling content was designed with business professionals like you in mind. The *Roadmap* series reveals all that you have ever wanted to know about performance, leadership, talent performance, management and optimizing your business strategies.

Natalie Manor
3101 Browns Mill Road, Suite 6-103
Johnson City, TN 37604
800-666-2230
www.The-Roadmap.com
www.NatalieManor.com
success@nataliemanor.com

ROADMAP to SUCCESS 9

An interview with...

Diane Bolden

David Wright (Wright)

Today we're talking with Diane Bolden. Diane is passionate about working with leaders to unleash human potential. With over sixteen years of experience in leadership and organization development, coaching, and consulting, Diane has worked with managers, directors and officers in organizations ranging from Fortune 500 companies to non-profits to achieve higher levels of performance and success by helping them bring out the best in themselves and everyone around them. Diane founded Synchronistics Coaching and Consulting with the mission of helping leaders and their organizations identify, develop, and apply their innate talent and untapped potential toward achieving extraordinary results.

Diane, welcome to *Roadmap to Success.*

Diane Bolden (Bolden)

Thank you for that gracious introduction. I'm very pleased to be here.

Wright

Tell us a little bit about your career path and how you came to be where you are now.

Bolden

I have to confess that through my childhood and early adulthood, I never knew exactly what I wanted to do with my life. In fact, I often envied people who seemed to have it all figured out. I think I changed my major in college three or four times. I thought about studying education for a while, then media, and then psychology. While a lot of areas fascinated me, I had trouble saying I knew exactly what I wanted to do. I finally decided on a major that the college called "interdisciplinary studies," which was basically a combination of three minors. The three minors I picked were English, Business, and Communication. I was interested in each and I believe that I use a lot of each in what I do, but at the time I had no idea what that was preparing me for.

After I graduated from college, I decided to pack up and leave my hometown. I moved to a place where I did not know anybody. I didn't have any job leads. I didn't even know where I was going to live. I just started looking for a job, an apartment, and friends. I ended up at an advertising agency and took a very entry-level job. Advertising sounded like fun and I figured it involves elements of communication, English, and certainly business. I was told that everybody starts at the bottom and gets promoted after a year and so I thought, what the heck?

I quickly found out that advertising was not my calling. I couldn't help noticing there was a lot of turnover, especially in the agency's entry-level positions. In fact, it was curious to me that they would recruit people who were at the top of their class with a lot of ambition and talent and these people, after a certain period of time, felt a lot like I did—under-utilized and uninspired. They were leaving in droves and the funny thing is that when the agency had an opportunity to promote somebody (as we were told would happen periodically), it didn't happen because we weren't really being prepared for moving up in the corporation. Instead, they brought in people from other agencies, which eroded any loyalty or trust that existed.

The longer I stayed, the more obvious it became to me that with the low morale of the employees, the customer often became almost an afterthought. I found that troubling. It just didn't seem as though the agency was achieving the success that it could and I thought it might be interesting to look into that a little bit. So I started interviewing people and asking them basic organizational questions. I asked: What do you think is going on with the organization? What do you think could be improved? What would it take to make you feel as though you were making a meaningful contribution here? I took notes and after a while I collected a lot of data. I researched the turnover costs and estimated the impact they were having on the business and I combined it all into a report.

I proposed a program that involved the more senior people teaching the younger people, who were hungry for knowledge. This would help the agency utilize their resources to grow their own talent, keep people stimulated and excited, build better loyalty, and get to know their customer.

I didn't have a very strong relationship with my boss at the time. In fact, I had a story in my head that she didn't like me very much (which in retrospect, was probably more of a story than anything), but it kept me from going to her with my idea. Being naïve and not yet really having grasped the chain of command concept, I went straight to the Vice President of Operations with my proposal. He was open and listened thoughtfully to it all. The agency ended up creating a position for me to head up the program I had proposed. When my boss found out about it she was, not surprisingly, very unhappy. She called on her networks and ultimately I was told that while they really liked my program and planned on implementing it, because of the controversy that was being generated they were not going to put me in the position of leading it.

I was devastated. I thought, oh my gosh, where do I go now? What am I going to do? Then I realized, hey wait a minute. Maybe I'm on to something here; maybe I can take this experience and do something with it. It was a little while before I discovered that there's a whole field out there called "organization development." The underlying premise is that of helping organizations identify the underlying dynamics that influence the results (or the lack of results) they are getting, and help them make adjustments to achieve more success.

With that, I started my career in training and development and over time I designed leadership development programs as an internal consultant for a handful of Fortune 500 Companies. I went back to school in the evenings and got an MBA. I began getting involved with teams and doing consulting and organizational development work, which included projects like strategic planning, group facilitation, total quality management, and team building. I became fascinated by human behavior and learning what it is that makes people and teams in organizations successful.

It became a routine part of my job to receive calls from leaders who would ask me to basically "fix" their people. They might tell me that their teams weren't getting the results they wanted or their people weren't doing what they wanted them to do. They would ask me to come in and teach them a class that would help their employees "perform."

I would go and talk with these people and ask the same questions I did in the ad agency to find out what they thought needed to change. I'd get a lot of feedback for the leader suggesting that while there were issues the people needed to take responsibility for, a lot of changes couldn't happen until the leader started taking responsibility. Perhaps the vision wasn't very clear and people didn't understand the expectations, or their roles were muddy and they were stepping on each other's toes. Or they didn't have the resources or the skills they needed and so the leader needed to take some responsibility for making a change.

The teams and their leaders would then create action plans identifying what steps they could commit to and we would follow-up three to six months later. But what I noticed was, even though a lot of these folks had really great intentions, their changes often didn't stick. They would revert back to old habits and patterns. Then I discovered a new field called coaching.

My boss at the time pulled me into his office one day and said, "You know, there's this new phenomenon going around called business coaching and I think we ought to become certified to do that." So I did and I really felt like that was the missing piece of the puzzle for me. Because what coaching allowed me to do was help people understand the underlying dynamics behind why they were getting the results, or the lack of results, that they were getting and how to shift their thoughts and behavior and take action to institute new patterns that would actually take root.

I've been doing that kind of work since early 2000. I've worked with hundreds of people, both in groups and workshops and one-on-one, and after awhile I started to notice some themes evolve around what helped people become more successful and what would keep them from that success. And now I feel compelled to share that with as many people as I can because I think the more people who know this, the better off everyone is going to be.

Wright

Why are you so passionate about leadership?

Bolden

When I look at organizations it strikes me that no matter what the goal is or what the organization is trying to do, it needs good people in order to make the right things happen. They can have all the greatest assets, the most amazing equipment, the most cutting-edge technology, the soundest strategies, and intellectual property, but if the company doesn't have people who can put all of those things together and utilize them in a way that gets results, it's not going to succeed. Each person has his own unique combination of talent, energy, style, and passion. I really think that true leaders are the ones who help people bring out their people's strengths and focus those strengths on getting results. I love leadership because of the potential it represents for organizations.

Then there is the other side of that, which is really about people themselves. I just can't believe how many of us seem to look at work as something to do to pass the time and bring home a paycheck. Many of us wake up Monday morning and work to get through the week so that we can do what we *really* want to do. So many people are tired at work, and yet, if ever there was a place that we could make a difference, if ever there was an arena in which we have the opportunity to take our own unique talent and channel it into something that is meaningful, it's within the organizations in which we work. We spend more of our waking hours at work than we do with our own families and friends. I think that leaders are in a unique position to be able to really see that potential in people and bring it out, often before they even recognize it in themselves. That's why I think strong leaders are so very critical.

Wright

What is your definition of a leader?

Bolden

It's funny because people often think of leaders as those who are in high profile positions within corporations—managers, directors or officers. In our communities we think of civic leaders or community leaders or political leaders. I certainly think all these people are leaders, but I also think that leaders are everywhere. I think that anybody who brings out the best in others and focuses that unique talent style, energy, and passion to accomplish something extraordinary is a leader. That's really my definition.

I believe leaders are also parents, coaches, teachers, community volunteers, politicians, healers, entertainers, writers, inventors, musicians, artists, and a myriad of people who are working in organizations without formal leadership titles, but who have influence on others and are in a position to help people bring out their best. So I think that leadership takes different forms. I think some people do well having people report to them or being at the helm of an organization. For others, leadership might take the form of developing new ideas and new ways of thinking or influencing people through artistic expression or some other creative endeavor.

Wright

So what then is the difference between management and leadership?

Bolden

I have seen studies that define management as planning, controlling, organizing, and directing. I think management can also be about keeping things the same and basically preventing all hell from breaking loose. It's keeping things functioning and orderly. I believe management is based in the head. It's very analytical and logical. But leadership is in the heart.

I think leadership is about connecting with people and inspiring them to do things that they may not have realized were possible, rather than maintaining the status quo as management tends to focus on. Leadership is about scanning the environment and looking for areas where the status-quo could be elevated—where something that hasn't been done before could be accomplished—and raising people's sights to see those possibilities and having the courage to take action to make the organization, the community, or even the world a better place. I think leadership is about getting results through people.

I think both managers and leaders are necessary, and I think that one without the other falls flat.

Wright

So what do you think makes a great leader?

Bolden

That's a fascinating question. I've asked people that question repeatedly—when they think of the greatest leaders, who comes to mind and why? It's always an interesting discussion because no matter what the answer is, it tends to be more focused on who people are rather than what they do. I'll hear descriptions of great leaders using terms such as, honest, authentic, sees the best in others, believes in people, visionary, trustworthy, courageous, direct, humble, not afraid to make mistakes, connects with people, makes others feel important, walks their talk—the list goes on and on.

I started my career teaching classes on subjects such as delegation, creating a vision, setting goals, providing feedback, resolving conflict, having difficult conversations, etc. What I realized over the years is that extraordinary leaders aren't necessarily the ones who have mastered all the techniques. They're the ones who have the ability to speak to our hearts as well as to our minds and awaken something in their people that is dormant and waiting to emerge. They're able to nurture and focus that into something that makes the organization a better place. I think that great leaders learn to do this for others by doing it for themselves first. And I don't think there's a step-by-step processes or a script that can be easily followed.

There is an age-old debate about whether leaders are born or made. I think it's a little bit of both. I think we come into the world with the bare essentials of everything we need to be successful, similar to a seed that contains the essence of everything it is destined to become. We then nurture those basic skills by our own unique experiences (both positive and the less than positive), by what we learn from those experiences, and by our relationships with people.

People have come to me to work on various issues over the years— building better relationships, improving their communication, working with difficult people, having greater influence or presence, making better decisions, building stronger teams, increasing productivity, etc., but underneath it all, what these people really seek to do is become more of who they truly are and tap into their own greatness so that it has it's own expression.

Michelangelo said, "The masterpiece is already in the marble," and I think the same is true of each and every one of us. I think that at the core, that's what leadership is about. I think that what makes leaders great is that they are authentic—they're tapping into their own greatness and in doing so can help others to do the same.

Wright

So how exactly does a leader go about becoming more of who he or she really is?

Bolden

I think each of us has our own unique roads and it's easy to think that if we just emulate the actions of others we're going to be more successful. There is certainly something to be gained by admiring folks and looking at what has worked for others. But my philosophy is that we tend to be drawn to people who have elements of the very qualities that we already have within ourselves. So the opportunity is not to emulate them; but rather, to find ways to tap into those qualities within yourself and give them your own unique expression. We have to be careful about trying to walk the path of another because when you do, you move further away from your own. I don't think you can lead by being someone you're not. Many have tried and I think people see through it. It's uninspiring and overblown and it takes a lot of energy that would be far better directed in other ways. When you compare yourself with others, it leads to frustration and self-defeating behaviors. The key is learning to recognize our greatness and to give it its own expression.

People who captivate us, whether they are performers or everyday people, are in their zone. They often seem to have a magical quality or spark; I think it's because they have found their own greatness and tapped into that. We are drawn to them because they represent what is possible for us. I think the thing that allows us to find that greatness is the unique combination of personal experiences each of us has had. There are going to be some successes and there are going to be some disappointments. When things go in directions we'd rather they didn't, it's very easy to wish those things away with thoughts like, "If only this would pass," or, "If this difficult person wasn't in my life anymore everything would be great."

I think true leaders tend to embrace all of these experiences and look at life as a workshop that gives them an opportunity to learn more about who they are and what they can bring out in themselves to meet their challenges. Rather than running from those challenges, if we experience them with awareness and look at what we can learn from each of them, whether the experience is successful or disappointing, we gain clues into who we are and what we're meant to do—and we often learn how to do it better next time.

I think there are a lot of things you can do to help connect the dots of your own experience. Something that I personally find helpful is journaling, because it allows you to tap into things on a subconscious level that you may not recognize when you're in everyday routines. Working with a coach can also be very helpful, as coaches are instrumental in helping people to look at themselves, others, and their experiences through new eyes. There are also several great programs out there designed to go beneath the surface and help you identify the ways in which you are getting in your own way so you can make the shifts necessary to achieve success.

I founded my company with the mission of offering programs like these to help people unearth their own talent, passion, and unique styles and do the same for others.

As we go about our daily lives, there are going to be times when we feel uncomfortable, anxious, or of out of sorts, and I think these feelings can be clues that something we believe is not consistent with who we are. It is not uncommon for some of the beliefs we've held to have successfully propelled us to a certain point, and then over time have diminishing returns. Often these old beliefs not only lose their effectiveness, but also become downright detrimental.

I call the times when things come to a head "defining moments." They require you to choose which belief or version of yourself you're going to be. Are you going to continue to think something or behave in a way that was successful for a while but is no longer true or are you going to change your definition into something that is more fitting with who you really are and align yourself with that?

Wright

Will you give us an example of one of your own defining moments?

Bolden

Sure. All my life I've been somewhat of an over-achiever, which I think can be a good thing—if it's healthy. But for a lot of my life it was unhealthy. I was compelled to over-excel in everything. I had to get straight A's. I was a member of just about every organization I could become a part of through high school and college, many of which I wasn't even that interested in. I felt I had to prove myself and I had a success formula in my head that said to succeed I needed to become the version of what I thought people wanted me to be. So I did all kinds of things that took me away from myself. I was, again not surprisingly, harried and stressed out all the time and really quite unfulfilled. After I got out of college that same success formula operated for me in the corporate world. I continued to try to identify what people did to get ahead and find a way to emulate them. It was not a very authentic way of being for me.

One of my most significant defining moments was being offered an opportunity to take a high profile job I thought I couldn't pass up. The position had more money, more authority, more acclaim—and required me to transition from some of the things I loved to do to get involved in activities that really were not my passion. Even the thought of doing the work involved turned my stomach. The activities took me away from working with and developing people to focus on areas that had no appeal to me.

But I went through the motions. Each time a book arrived on a new topic I needed to learn about, I became nauseous. I began to have a hard time sleeping and I didn't want to get out of bed in the morning. One day I realized that I had convinced myself that I had no choice but to take this position because it was part of the success formula I had created for myself in my head. I believed I needed to become that version of whoever somebody thought I needed to be to succeed and it just wasn't working for me anymore.

So in that critical moment I had the choice to decide who I was going to be. I could continue to play into something that was far more fitting for somebody else or I could take a leap into something that was scary, but felt much more stimulating, inspiring, and exciting to me. And in those moments, I created a new success formula for myself—to succeed I must be myself in all situations. This was one of my most liberating moments because I ended up stepping down from my position and focused all my energy into following my bliss, as the legendary Joseph Campbell advocates. This has truly made all the difference in the world. I wouldn't be here having this conversation with you, writing and teaching and working with others in the way that I am now if I hadn't done that.

Wright

Is that what led you to start your own business?

Bolden

Yes, I think it set the wheels in motion. I had always dreamed of having my own business and finally got to the point where I knew it was something I had to do. I had also come to a critical juncture where I knew that the work in the organization I was a part of would take me in a direction that was no longer aligned with where I wanted to go. The other critical factor in my decision was my three children, who were quite young at the time. They are such a big part of who I am and what I do; I wanted to have the flexibility to spend more time with them. I felt that starting my own business would allow me to do that while doing work I love. I believe I am a better mother and wife when I am doing work that fulfills me.

A lot of people thought I was nuts. I had what many people would consider to be an enviable position. A couple of colleagues who I greatly respect sat me down and read me the riot act. They told me about other colleagues they'd known who had gone off on their own and failed miserably. They warned me that someday I would regret such a decision. These discussions had an impact on me. They led me to question, "How can I know that what I'm doing is right?"

And I obsessed about that question. Then one day I was out running on a path where people often train for 10Ks and marathons. There was a mile marker with a quote underneath it. It said, "Those who say it cannot be done should get out of the way of those who are doing it." The hair on my arms just stood up. I knew this silly sign was my answer. I used to think that you needed to create a vision of who you wanted to become and then work really hard to make it happen. But now I realize that when you get quiet, pay attention, and connect the dots of your unique combination of experiences, your vision has a way of finding you. And when it does, there's nothing left for you to do but act on it.

Wright

Your definition of leadership centers on bringing out the best in others. Would you tell our readers how leaders go about doing that?

Bolden

Well, I think they need to start by bringing out the best in themselves, as we've talked about previously. The other thing I think they need to do is pay attention to what they're focusing on. It's really easy to become preoccupied with things that we're dissatisfied with—obstacles we're encountering, fears and frustrations, and the perceived limitations of ourselves and others. I believe it's true in many ways that you get what you focus on. So if you're focused on things that keep you steeped in your problems, you're going to continue to see more of them.

I think this dynamic is true with our view of others, too. When we focus on their seeming weaknesses or lack of confidence or perhaps the rough edges that they haven't quite polished yet, people will tend to show us more of those things. We end up drawing out uncertainties in others that can sometimes lead them to focus on their doubts and negatively influence their confidence and performance. This is especially prone to happen when we are frustrated or angry with others and it occupies our thoughts with all the ways in which they are annoying us. Whether consciously or not, when our minds are focused on such things, we end up acting in ways that bring out more of the behavior we don't want to see.

I believe the wonderful thing is that the converse is also true—we can also bring out the best in others by what we choose to focus on. We can choose to focus on people's redeeming qualities and potential and what we respect and admire in them. And there is always something positive to find there. When you look into the areas of people's beings that are confident and resourceful and well intentioned, I think people surprise you. I've seen it time and time again. People live up to our expectations—not what we hope they will do, but what we know in our hearts they have the ability to do.

In any given moment we can focus on limitations or potential. This is not a new concept. Henry Ford said, "Whether you think you can, or you think you cannot, you're right." Harvey McKay said, "Optimists are right and so are pessimists. It's up to you to decide what you will be." You can be the kind of person who makes others feel like they can't do anything wrong, that they are amazing, that they have unlimited potential or you can be the kind of person who intimidates folks and drives out their insecurities and causes them to fixate on something that is unproductive. You always have the choice.

We can also lead people to focus and grow from their experiences and their opportunities. We can influence people to focus on the problem or we can influence them to focus on the solution; by our own example we can raise the sights of others. What a wonderful opportunity for leaders! You have the ability to truly bring out the best in folks and help them to see things in themselves they may have not even seen, and bring it out. Through your interaction, you can create a space where they can try new behaviors, feeling as though there is somebody who believes in them, who is going to see beyond their less than desirable behavior into their true capabilities and help them succeed.

Wright

So who are some of the leaders you admire most?

Bolden

There are several actually. Mahatma Gandhi is one of the primary ones. Through his teachings he showed us that we have to be the change we want to see. Merriam Webster defines a leader as someone who guides others on a path by going on ahead. I think Gandhi showed us what that means. Leading the way doesn't mean you tell everybody where to go and what to do. It means that you go first—you show people—you are the example, and through your example others will the way to rise.

Ralph Waldo Emerson is another person I truly admire. He may not fit many people's formal definition of a leader, but his writings and teachings have stood the test of time. They have influenced countless others to find the best in themselves and bring it out. His messages are about self-reliance; they help us understand that we all need to march to our own drummer—we can accomplish things in the world just by being who we truly are.

Franklin Delano Roosevelt was another amazing leader. He certainly had his own personal struggles, but during a time when our country was sinking into depression, both financially and spiritually, he rose up to aggressively attack the challenges confronting the nation. People were despondent and hopeless and yet he was able to focus their energy into something constructive and regenerating. He did the same when the country was drawn into the Second World War.

Oprah Winfrey is an interesting example of an extraordinary current day leader. She showcases people's strong spirits wherever she goes and in whatever she does. She is not put off by challenges. In fact, she deliberately seeks out people who are dealing with their challenges in remarkable ways and holds them up as examples. She sets wonderful examples through her own work as well. All of this helps people to focus on stories of hope, inspiration, and success that allow us all to remember what we're capable of. She brings positive thought into the world and I think that's huge.

I also love Herb Kelleher. He has mastered the art of truly connecting with the people he leads and allows them to be part of his creation. He never tries to be somebody he's not. In fact, he embraces his quirkiness; I think that endears him to others. He makes people feel good about who they are and then inspires them to elevate the status of his organization, not because he tells them to or because that's their job, but because it's something that they want to do. He creates an organization that people are proud to be a part of, and I really think that spills over to their customers. Southwest Airlines has countless customers who repeatedly choose that airline because of the way the airline's employees make them feel.

Wright

What closing advice would you give to leaders, both old and new?

Bolden

There are three distinct components that we need to keep balanced to truly bring out our own greatness in a way that inspires and empowers others. These three areas include knowledge, thought, and action. Any one of these by themselves is going to fall flat.

Often leaders possess a great deal of knowledge that they are unable to effectively act on. One of the primary reasons is that their thinking gets in the way. As an example, let's say you're trying to give somebody feedback. If you have an underlying assumption that telling people what you really think is going to damage the relationship or discourage them or have some other negative consequence, it doesn't matter how skilled you are at giving feedback. You're probably not going to do it as well and proactively as you otherwise could. So you've got to become aware of the beliefs you have about what it is you're trying to do and make any necessary shifts *before* you can really integrate your knowledge. Then, of course, you have to act on it. This introduces an element of risk and sometimes requires you to go out of your comfort zone. You may make mistakes and things may not go the way you want them to right out of the chute. But every time you integrate your knowledge and thought with action, you'll learn something new about yourself that will take you to a higher plane. And as you continue to evolve, the contributions you can make as a leader will increase.

I would also tell leaders new and old to never second-guess themselves. Don't ever underestimate the impact you can have wherever you are. Leaders are often in unique positions where they have the ability to influence large numbers of people. Even if it just starts with one person—you may impact that person in a way that allows him or her to go out and inspire others— whether it's dozens, hundreds, or hundreds of thousands. Maybe that one person helps one other person; the effects of that are exponential.

I would also say don't get caught up in comparing yourself to others. Realize that you have something extraordinary to bring to the world and so does every single person who surrounds you. We need to find a way to see that uniqueness in ourselves and in others and then bring it out.

Take action in spite of your fears. Learn from your mistakes. Be yourself. And do it now. The world needs you.

Wright

What a great conversation. I really do appreciate all the time you've taken to answer these questions. I have learned a tremendous amount here and I'm sure our readers will as well.

Bolden

Thank you.

Wright

Today we've been talking with Diane Bolden. Diane has worked with managers, directors, and officers in organizations ranging from Fortune 500 companies to non-profits to achieve higher levels of performance and success by helping them bring out the best in themselves and everyone around them. I think we've found out today how she does it.

Diane, thank you so much for being with us today on *Roadmap to Success*.

Bolden

Thank you very much. It was truly a pleasure.

About the Author

Diane Bolden founded Synchronistics Coaching & Consulting with the mission of helping leaders and their organizations identify, develop, and apply their innate talent and untapped potential toward achieving extraordinary results. She is author of *The Seven Secrets of Extraordinary Leaders* and *Ten Traps Leaders Set for Themselves—and How to Avoid Them* and creator of numerous programs designed to help leaders unleash the extraordinary in themselves and others.

Diane is passionate about working with leaders to unleash human potential. With over sixteen years of experience in leadership and organization development, coaching, and consulting, Diane has worked with managers, directors, and officers in both Fortune 500 and nonprofit companies to achieve higher levels of performance and success by helping them to bring out the best in themselves and everyone around them.

Diane is happily married and blessed with three beautiful children.

Diane M. Bolden, Founder/President
Synchronistics Coaching & Consulting, LLC
4148 N. Arcadia Drive
Phoenix, AZ 85018
Phone: 602.889.2329
E-mail: Diane@DianeBolden.com
www.UnleashTheExtraordinary.com

10

An interview with...

Don Deems

David Wright (Wright)

Dr. Deems' life passion is assisting people to find freedom, peace, and fulfillment in their life and work. He helps clients discover obstacles that limit creativity and power and helps them develop skills and abilities to create collaborative relationships and to learn cutting-edge leadership skills through personal coaching, retreats, and workshops for teams and their leaders looking to maximize their potential and overcome self-defeating patterns. He gives presentations and workshops on topics related to personal and professional growth and offers original publications and newsletters. The only dentist recipient of the American Psychological Association's National Best Practices Honors, Dr. Deems has received extensive awards and honors for his professional work.

Dr. Deems, welcome to *Roadmap to Success.*

Dr. Don Deems (Deems)

Thanks David, it's great to be here.

Wright

From your experience both as a business owner and a professional business coach, what do you find as the single most important reason more people don't experience success and fulfillment in their work and their life?

Deems

That's a great question and it seems to really be at the crux of everything. My experience has been that the reason for less than successful business experience usually boils down to one thing and it's not what you might think it is! I've witnessed many people with drive and enthusiasm that failed. I've even seen well-read business owners who thought they'd covered all the bases never to achieve the success they wanted. I've watched owners spend countless dollars on consultants only to see little to no lasting change. I've even seen businesses bring in motivational speakers to rally its troops only to see the enthusiasm wither away with the next challenge or unresolved problem.

What usually gets in the way of business success—and for that matter success in life—is the person: his or her level of personal growth and self-defeating behaviors. We can all learn techniques, methodologies, and principles of running a business, and we can devise elaborate systems to run efficiently and effectively. We can even hire the best and the brightest to help us get organized, but if we don't make the investment in what I believe is the most important thing—the investment in ourselves—we just won't experience the freedom, vitality, and success in our life and our life's work.

Wright

With all of the available technology, research, and money available, what's your opinion as to why the United States is fifth in productivity compared to all other nations?

Deems

That's amazing isn't it? We're supposed to be this greatly prosperous country yet we just are not very productive, relatively speaking. We all may have opinions about why that might be, such as work ethics or values or management styles, and these and other things can certainly contribute to this decreased productivity. From my perspective, one of the biggest reasons that our productivity is so low is stress—that ubiquitous, overused term that describes all the pressures of life that we have to deal with, especially workplace stress. Stress at the workplace ranks near the top, as evidenced by the large volume of information about stress available to us today.

For example, many clients I work with have very high levels of stress, both at work and at home, and dealing with that stress seems to be a full time job; thus the reason for escape from that stress, whether it's with food, alcohol, religion, or any number of distractions. What clients want is relief from their stress! Business owners want relief, employees want relief, everyone wants relief. Stress takes its toll on business in terms of lost and decreased productivity, increased turnover, absenteeism, poor loyalty, job dissatisfaction, and lack of cooperation among team members.

Of course, this also affects the employee and the business owner much the same, except it's a personal experience for both the employee and the business owner. These personal experiences take the form of illnesses, increased number of visits to the doctor, and alcohol and substance abuse, among others. Overcoming stress in the workplace is a different matter and one that doesn't necessarily take a lot of money, but requires definite awareness and focus on what it takes to decrease stress in the workplace.

For example, one of the simplest ways to reduce stress in the workplace is learning exceptional communication skills. As simple as that sounds, the lack of communication skills I encounter in businesses is amazing, whether it's among employees or between the business owner and the employees. Of course we all think we know how to communicate, don't we? Although exceptional communication can be a very complicated process due to the wide variety of experiences, values, agendas, issues, concerns, and problems that each and every one of us have, achieving that is also the most rewarding in terms of what it can do for the business.

When I conduct workshops, I feel tremendous joy watching teams learn how to communicate effectively. Their faces light up, there's connection among team member and business owner/managers, there's no more walking around issues that may have plagued the team for years. Morale is boosted and people feel empowered to finally discuss matters that mean the most to them. Ultimately, this results in increased productivity for the team—and the business. Even better, people take these new skills home with them, and their relationships at home improve too.

Wright

How did you become a professional coach, coming from a background in professional dentistry?

Deems

Many people ask me that very question because it's an odd combination—being a dentist and a coach. The short answer is that my interest peaked after I had worked with other coaches, although coaching wasn't necessarily recognized as the profession it is today. I had been in private practice for about seven years when my partner committed suicide. I was left $600,000 in debt to his estate and that didn't include my personal debts. Prior to working with my first coach I had been doing what most business owners do, which is to learn by trial and error, but now I was really in major overwhelm. I needed help!

Getting through my situation was complicated. I had a family to take care of, including two small children, I felt emotionally dead, and I dreaded going to work because that's all that I could do—there was no other option.

Most days I felt sick to my stomach about it. My stress level was through the roof and in response to the situation I developed some very poor coping mechanisms. I stayed really angry most of the time. The relationships I had with people were poor, and I was not living in my own integrity. I had a lot of technical knowledge and skills about my business, but I had minimal skills at anything else needed to run a successful business. You can see that life wasn't very fun for me at that time!

Fortunately, I decided to get help. I read a lot of books and attended personal growth retreats and workshops. I learned communication and people skills. I focused on my personal development, and I kept building on my professional training. Most importantly, I worked with coaches and consultants.

It was through this process over many years that I discovered how much I enjoyed helping other people overcome their own challenges and have the life they've always wanted. That led me into reading some books about coaching, and eventually I completed my training as a professional coach. It has been a joy and a privilege to be a coach to others. Coaching is truly my passion, so I am so grateful now to be in that position of helping other people through many of the same problems and concerns and issues that I faced. To work with other people is the greatest gift I've been given.

My focus in coaching has been working with solo professionals primarily because I am one and because I know the intricate details and the challenges that being a solo business owner can bring. It's a very complicated thing because solo business owners have to wear so many different hats each day. It's a challenge for many business owners just to keep treading water sometimes, much less be successful, and it's even more challenging to experience the freedom, rewards, and satisfaction that being a solo business owner can bring.

To experience all of those positive things (and these are the things that draw people into becoming a business owner in the first place) it requires a lot of skill and talents. There usually isn't much time to learn them when you have to keep the business going or when you've got to stop a downward slide into business failure. Just to reiterate a point I made earlier, having technical training and business knowledge is important when being a business owner, although having that knowledge won't do you any good if you can't effectively lead your team and your business. Leading requires great communication and relationship skills.

My journey into learning so many of these things came through the help of coaches and consultants, by far. In fact, it really sped the process up for me. I feel that the value of the one-on-one interaction between a coach and client is a powerful way to work very effectively toward success, both personally and professionally.

Wright

With a plethora of self-help books, both business and personal, why do you feel professionals don't generally achieve the success they so greatly desire and have put their hearts and souls into achieving?

Deems

I believe more people don't experience this success and fulfillment in owning a business because owning a business is such a multi-faceted challenge. You just can't have great technical skills; you can't just have great listening skills. There's so much that's needed for a business to be successful. There is not an easy way, because if there was, it would not be a problem for anyone to have a successful business! And because business is not a one-size-fits-all way, many owners get lost in this plethora of information available to them—it's very frustrating!

I know from my earlier experiences that I tried lots of things, and I tried to emulate lots of people and lots of businesses. What I found out was that I had to find my *own* way, take what I could learn from other people, trust my own intuition, build on my experiences, and develop myself as a person. Most importantly, I found out that I couldn't do it alone—I needed help. In fact, I needed a *village* of people to help me navigate the waters of running a business.

By working with my own coach, I was able to sift through the personally relevant information much faster, gain a focus on my strengths, and make some significant paradigm shifts in the way I approached life and business. It can be like a maze doing it alone, which is one of the big reasons people get stuck and sometimes even paralyzed in their growth. They hear so much information that it becomes hard for them to determine what's best for them and their business. By working with someone who could help me see the bigger picture, it was easier to make some real progress without getting stuck. I ended up doing it many times faster than if I had tried to do it alone. Besides the fact that trying to figure it out alone was cumbersome and expensive, there was also the personal side of development. Let me explain.

Business owners are intelligent, hardworking, well-intentioned people with much of the same concerns and life issues that you and I have. However, these concerns and issues tend to be amplified when we're the business owner. Thus, the business owner's personal development becomes absolutely paramount. It's not that psychological help is needed, it's that weaknesses in our own level of personal development become exposed more often and more vigorously because we're the business owner and the leader; we're the ones whom employees look to for guidance and direction.

To help the business succeed during challenging times, a strong personal foundation is needed, so I encourage business owners to make their personal development equally as important as any other area of growth and development in their business.

Wright

If you were to discuss the most valuable traits of a leader, what would you say they are and why?

Deems

There are probably a thousand books on that topic, aren't there? For me it really boils down to the person. People's connection with their heart, their soul, their needs, their values, their ability to effectively communicate and relate to others, their ability to set large boundaries and adhere to high standards in their own life: these are at the core of the issue of what constitutes the traits of a good leader. In short, I think it's their ability to "walk their talk," so to speak. People look up to people who are strong and focused; they want to work with people who will listen and support them. They want to be able to understand clearly what the leader is trying to accomplish and how they can best contribute to that, so a leader has to do all that and even more. I would certainly include other traits, such as being visionary, maintaining consistency and focus, creating accountability, and being accountable.

Other attributes that leaders would benefit from include having charisma, confidence, honesty, sincerity, integrity, and right action. With the pace of business these days being what it is, being forward- looking is absolutely key in today's business environment, or you'll get left behind. Being able to set goals and having some sort of vision for the business' future is critical. Displaying the confidence in all you do is a must, but what do you do if you have self-defeating behaviors that don't allow that to happen? Again, it's the level of personal growth and development that shows up.

I've worked with many clients whose only roadblock to success was self-defeating behaviors, so once those are recognized we can work through those behaviors and become much more successful and focused. Again, growing personally and professionally is not an option for a business owner and leader. By showing commitment and endurance in the intellectual, mental, physical, and spiritual development, leaders inspire others to reach new heights.

The good news is that business owners and people in leadership positions, whether by choice or not, can become great leaders. However, they can't learn this by only being in a classroom or by reading a book. A place where they learn to be that great leader is in everyday life, in the entanglement of dealing with the challenges and successes that come about through living and working. The real key is developing the awareness, self-confidence, and highly effective problem-solving skills to meet those challenges. This is the experience that I call personal growth.

Wright

You've had a life of extreme business challenges and adversities. How has that molded you?

Deems

Yes, the ups and downs have been pretty horrendous, but that's just been my path and fortunately you don't need to experience those big swings in order to be on the road to success! For me, the major personal business challenges molded me into who I am because they required me to develop the personal awareness, self-confidence, and reliance on my knowledge, skills, and intuition to get through whatever came up.

I had to develop an attitude of being willing to learn—and even wanting to learn—and to not avoid concerns, issues, and limits that can stifle progress. I had to learn what sustains me from the inside out in times of trial and tribulation so that I could keep going, even when I felt tired, beaten, and bruised. I had to know if I was willing to get up the next morning and face the day with an intention of getting comfortable with that which I couldn't see or predict, or the failures I couldn't seem to bear. In short, I had to learn who I was. It's hard to teach that to anyone. I mean, how would you teach that to anyone?

I encourage people who want to be successful to not shrink back from trials and tribulations, to stay true to their course in times of success or failure, to listen to their critics, to learn from their mistakes, and to be open to all possibilities. To do that, one must develop a keen awareness of human behavior.

Let me give you an example. At one time, I was primarily consumed with my own problems, fears, and issues, and that made me very inwardly focused in a negative way. What people *felt* was the furthest thing from my mind, and that was *disastrous* for my business. Eventually it led me to being sued—twice. Although my attorneys felt I did nothing wrong, I knew I had: I hadn't developed the relationship with these patients the way I should have. I was too focused on my own problems and concerns to pay attention to their problems and concerns. Effectively, I was convinced I was right and they were wrong. I was afflicted with the only terminal disease known to mankind, which I call righteousness. It is defined as thinking that you're right with no possibility of being wrong. It was terrible, and I didn't—and couldn't—see it. Not only was I *not* growing, I wasn't doing much of anything right. It was really a bad time.

The challenges I've faced have also molded me in terms of being a real student of leadership and business. As I mentioned earlier, I incurred this huge debt when my business partner committed suicide, and all of a sudden I was holding all the marbles and I didn't have a clue what to do with them! At first I did what I thought was the right thing to do—I just worked harder and harder. After all, that's what I had learned to that point in my life about business. So again, I just dug in and worked even harder, many times over seventy plus hours a week.

Eventually, my body and spirit started to suffer from all the strain, and I knew things had to change for me to be able to survive. Finally I asked for some help. I wanted to learn not just how to run a business better but also how to have a great life in the process. It was then I discovered that who we are personally actually makes the biggest impact on our business.

It's not just the systems, the planning skills, the leadership skills, or a strong work ethic—it's who we *are* that matters most. I encourage everyone to ask for help whatever their situation, whether they're in danger of losing a business or they're just looking to grow and develop a great business further. Going it alone is tough, and very few people make it that way.

Wright

You're a professional coach; how does that differ from other similar professions, such as consulting or psychotherapy? And, why would someone choose coaching versus other modalities?

Deems

That's a great question because the three are linked. Consulting and psychotherapy are two closely compared professions because coaching grew out of the need for something in between the two. Many people came to the coaching profession having had previous careers as consultants or therapists. The simplest explanation I can give that would compare these three modalities of learning would go something like this: If I were a consultant, and you came to me and wanted to learn to ride a bike, I might show you a bike. I might explain how all the components work together and how to repair it. I might explain the laws of momentum and discuss the variations possible in bike construction. That might be all that you need to know to pick up that bike and start riding, and then again, maybe not. Regardless, the information is valuable in many ways.

If I were a therapist, I might approach your learning to ride a bike based on your past experiences trying to ride a bike or just trying to learn something new. We might explore the fears that keep you from riding a bike or even explore past experiences that may have occurred that might prevent you from getting on a bike, maybe due to previous falls or injuries when trying to learn or do something new. Again this is very helpful and useful information, and it might be all that's needed for you to get on that bike.

As a coach, I'll ask you to sit on the bike, put your feet on the pedals, and start pedaling. I'll hold on to the seat while you experience learning to ride so that you don't fall, and when you're ready, you'll tell me to let go, and you'll be riding. I'll always be around to help when needed, and I'll be cheering you on the whole way. It's that simple, yet it's *that* powerful.

Choosing coaching is a very hands-on approach to learning. Not only do you learn to trust you own inner knowledge, you're also learning to draw on your own experiences. This allows you to learn to trust yourself, develop the confidence that's needed to succeed, and learn that it's smart to ask for help.

Coaching is a very powerful way to grow, develop, and learn. Over 25 percent of the Fortune 500 Companies know this and employ personal coaches for their top-level managers and executives. That number continues to grow each year, especially as more people experience personal and business coaching.

Wright

Many people who have heard of coaching associate it with "life design" or "life coaching." How is what you do similar or dissimilar from this?

Deems

Coaching originally developed out of a niche for people looking for help in an area of their life that they weren't able to find the right guidance in, which was their personal life. Initially, these were people who really didn't need therapy or counseling, but who were looking to work with somebody to grow their life in a more abundant way. They sought out people we now call coaches. So, it is both "life design" and "life coaching."

Because the coaching *process* is so powerful, coaches and people being coached began seeing the direct application to business. Because success in business is greatly determined by who we are as a person, utilizing a coach is now a natural fit for people who are not only looking for a great life, but to also have a great business. Coaching not only develops the person from the inside out but also from the outside in by developing awareness of our thoughts and actions and by becoming self-generating and self-correcting. We can become long- term, excellent performers in every area of our life. This is the essence of what coaching helps people do in their business and in their life.

In essence, my work as a professional coach encompasses all three: life design, life coaching, and business coaching.

Wright

Does personal growth and professional growth go hand-in-hand? Or can one focus on just one or the other?

Deems

They absolutely go hand-in-hand! I think we can all relate to knowing people who are incredibly brilliant and talented in their area of expertise, but whose lives are less-than-desirable or who are people we don't necessarily want to interact with. In the health professions, we have some incredibly smart people who know their specialty, but they lack the personal skills to have a successful business and, in my opinion, a successful life. There's so much emphasis on learning the facts, doing the research, and honing the skills needed for technical performance. Unfortunately, practically all of the communication and relationship skills—what I include under personal development—is left out. That's a *big* mistake, in my opinion.

The most successful people I know have become experts both professionally and personally, and they have great businesses and great lives to prove it. I don't recommend focusing on just one area or the other; a balanced approach is warranted. There is a business to run, and yes, we can't ignore that. However, if the focus is only on the areas needed to keep the business afloat, some troubled waters are ahead. Eventually the business and its owner can't hold up to the pressure and demands placed on them. We see many professionals who appear to have great businesses—and we *assume* great lives—and it seems that all of a sudden everything falls apart for them. What happened? In my experience, it was a lack of a strong personal foundation. I encourage people to grow in both arenas and not just focus on business development or personal development.

Wright

For a business owner who is looking for ways to experience greater success—or even turn their business around—what do you feel are the key areas to focus?

Deems

I'd suggest several areas of focus, and these are going to be areas that you may not have heard or read about very often. For starters—and this may even seem a little counter-intuitive—I suggest focusing on what's really working well. These are called our strengths. Our culture seems to be consumed with focusing on our weaknesses and what it takes to overcome them. The *problem* is *the focus*—the focus is on the weaknesses. When you focus on strengthening your strengths, the weaknesses eventually just disappear. As I said, it sounds counter-intuitive because of everything we read and are exposed to, but it's absolutely true in my experience. Success does breed success. By focusing on strengths, success comes much more quickly than by focusing on what's not working.

For example, the New Year is the time when many businesses and people make resolutions for the coming year. By definition, a resolution is a *resolve against* doing something. That's the wrong approach. The focus is all wrong. Of course, how many people actually have a resolution that was fulfilled? In my experience, not many people experience that. I'd suggest to you that if the resolution "worked," it was because the approach wasn't a traditional approach to a resolution. In reality, it probably was never a resolution—it was a positive intention to move in a life-affirming, business-affirming direction. Make positive, affirming statements; avoid the negative ones. Get rid of the resolutions!

Additionally, another key focus is what I call personal foundation. By personal foundation, I mean the foundation on which we live and base our lives and run our businesses. These components include things such as creating high standards, broadening our personal boundaries, building reserves, eliminating things that we put up with, completing all our unresolved matters, restoring our personal integrity, clarifying our values, getting our needs met, strengthening our family and our community, and restating our life and business and affirmations. It's a lot, isn't it? You can see this is a huge area of focus and one that may take a tremendous amount of time and effort. Fortunately, the payoffs are huge. And, there's no better person than a coach to work with in this area.

Alternatively, making the effort to develop a strong personal foundation maybe too lengthy a process for someone whose business may be a high risk of failure unless something is not done quickly. Businesses must be profitable or they'll sink. If you're in this situation, you'll want to get rid of what is not working and only keep those things that are working and build on those.

You might notice that this is also similar to and opposite of what we hear and read all the time—to never give up. I've seen too many people who never give up, when the best thing that they could have done is to stop doing what they were doing and just go in a different direction. Knowing when to do that is very important. I'm not saying that we should give up at the first sign of resistance, but instead I suggest paying close attention to what's taking place. Are there fundamental problems that can't be overcome without great cost? Are there small changes in your approach to tackling these obstacles that could be taken? What can be predicted about the current course you are taking? The most successful people I know are *not* the ones who persevered at all costs; they're the ones who paid attention and made necessary changes to insure success along the way. However, people *have* never given up and continue on their initial course and they eventually succeed. However, I would ask, what was the cost of persevering against all odds? There was probably great cost. I suggest there is a better way.

Wright

You have mentioned on several occasions the importance of relationship and connection. Why do you feel these are so important to success in business and in life?

Deems

I believe that everything we do is about connection—connection to each other, connection to our hearts, and connection to our environment. To be in connection is to be in relationship. I hope you hear that I'm not talking about networking or marketing or making friends and acquaintances, all of which are important for a business and *are* an aspect of connection. One of the reasons that many businesses are so successful is *because of* connection. It is the connection to their clients in a meaningful way, not just understanding their clients' preferences.

Conversely, many businesses aren't as successful because of their lack of connection to their clients and to their community. These days it's not just good enough to have a good product or service; to be truly successful you have to be involved. In a world of product and service availability literally at our fingertips, what will differentiate your business from someone else's? I would suggest to you it is connection. We live in a world where people are starving for intimacy, and I'm not speaking of intimacy as it relates to emotional or sexual intimacy. I'm speaking of intimacy as it relates to close connection to someone of similar values, interests, and concerns. People want to be heard and understood; they want to feel connected. Even as our world is getting more crowded and we have cell phones, the Internet, and cable television, most people don't feel connected. Your business can be more successful than you imagine if you tap into this unmet need.

I also speak of connection in a way that means more than just with your business's clients. I talk of connection from leader and owner to the employees and associates, connection to the business's vendors and suppliers, connections of employees to each other, all the way down to the person's connection with who he or she is personally. Connect all the dots and you've got a great business; don't connect the dots and you've got a bunch of loose parts. Truly, in both the largest and smallest sense, connection is the key to making business and life happen.

Further, I hope it's obvious from what I've said earlier, that all this connecting can't happen very effectively without the skills, awareness, focus, and development on *who* we are as people and as individuals.

Wright

What is different about your approach from others in the self-help community?

Deems

In short, my approach doesn't exclude the person from the business. The two are intertwined, so why try to separate them? There has to be this consistency and congruency between the two. You can't have professional growth without the personal growth to support it, or you end up with the proverbial "house of cards." It doesn't do any good to learn valuable management skills unless you have that personal foundation to carry them out. We all know of or have worked for a person in a managerial position whose life was in shambles and they kept trying to implement some management strategies with their non-existent relationship skills with little to no success. Having one set of skills without the other is disastrous, so I work with people on both levels at the same time. They experience success much more quickly this way without the huge upswings and the eventual downturns. If a strong foundation is built along the way, all the pieces come together to create something really *powerful,* which is a strong person and a strong business.

Wright

With all the "growth/success" publications, tapes and videos produced and sold over the last several decades, why hasn't there been an explosion of success stories? Or has there been?

Deems

Unfortunately about 80 percent of all small businesses in the United States are still going to fail in their first five years, and this hasn't changed much in recent years. In my opinion, we haven't seen an explosion of success stories at all. From my experience, it goes back to the person in charge of the business, specifically what's going on in his or her life. Does the person have the skills to start a business? Is it the right time in his or her life to own a business? Does the person really have the capital needed? Is the business set up for profitability from opening day? Certainly there are key areas for any businessperson to follow, but I have a few extra that I think are even more important than common knowledge and business acumen.

The first is creating a business around experiencing profit at a very low sales point. This includes being profitable and profit-driven from the opening day of business rather than becoming profitable after several years of loss or "investment." I encourage people to trash the old ideas of thinking you have to invest for a long period of time before you enjoy the sweet smell of success. It may be hard to imagine, but it can be done. Early profits allow you to create opportunity for even more profits.

Second, the business owner must have personal balance. Although balance isn't a term I normally like to use, it does give you the concept perhaps in a different way than how I've expressed it earlier. This does include aspects I've already mentioned such as strong personal foundation and attention to personal growth and development. It also includes items such as a plan to become financially independent and having habits that attend to personal, emotional, and physical needs.

Third, the business workplace must be conducive to employee involvement and recognition, work-life balance, health and safety, and employee growth and development. Employees *are* people; they have the same needs as the business owner—as you and I have. Make healthy workplace practices at the top of your business priority list and implement procedures and policies to make them affective.

Fourth, stay more intimately connected with your business's clients and their values and goals. Connection is everything; stay connected with your clients. Grow yourself to be *able* to connect with others in a deeper, more meaningful way, not just with surveys or customer appreciation days or other less meaningful methods of connection.

Fifth, make it important to make sure the business employees have all the equipment and training to double their productivity that other similar businesses already experience. If you're not sure what's needed, just ask them! Meet with them; support their growth, even if it means they ultimately leave your business because they've outgrown you or the business. By being 100 percent committed to their growth and success, your own business will experience success, too.

And lastly, I would recommend adding value to every service or product your business offers, whether your clients ask for them or not. Surprise them; make them proud to be associated with your business. Keep your workplace fresh and appealing. And, never take your clients for granted.

Wright

What a great conversation and what an enlightening conversation! I really appreciate the time you've taken to answer all these questions. I know I've learned a lot, and I'm sure our readers and listeners will too.

Deems

Thanks David, it's been great being with you.

Wright

Today we've been talking with Dr. Don Deems. Dr. Deems helps people discover obstacles that limit creativity and power, develop skills and build them to create collaborative relationships and learn cutting-edge leadership skills through his personal coaching. I think he knows what he's talking about!

Thank you so much, Dr. Deems, for being with us today on *Roadmap to Success.*

Deems

Thanks, David!

About the Author

Dr. Don Deems' life passion is assisting others to find freedom, peace, and fulfillment in their life and their work. As a professional personal and business coach, Dr. Deems helps others discover obstacles that limit their creativity and power, develop the skills and abilities to create co-creative, collaborative relationships, and learn cutting-edge leadership skills that empower both them and the people that work with them. He works with clients in the following ways: 1) one-on-one personal coaching, 2) facilitating personalized retreats for teams looking to maximize their potential, overcome self-defeating patterns, and expand their vision, 3) delivering keynote presentations and workshops on a variety of topics related to personal and professional growth, and 4) numerous articles published in professional journals, books, and his monthly coaching newsletter. Dr. Deems focuses his work primarily on healthcare and solo professionals, and has coached accountants, small business owners, coaches, therapists, and managers of small organizations. The only dentist recipient the American Psychological Association's National Best Practices Honors, Dr. Deems has received extensive awards and honors for his professional work.

Dr. Don Deems
12921 Cantrell Road, Suite 101
Little Rock, AR 72223
501-663-9903
Cell: 501-413-1101
www.drdondeems.com

An interview with...

Lorraine Grubbs

David Wright (Wright)

Today we are talking to Lorraine Grubbs. She is passionate about introducing companies to proven concepts that heighten the level of workforce loyalty. This philosophy espouses that loyal, engaged employees will be more productive, happier, and feel more fulfilled in the workplace, hence becoming owners of their own business. This ultimately translates into treating their external customers the same way, thus improving the bottom line. Lorraine spent fifteen years with the most successful airline in the world, Southwest Airlines. After writing her book, *Lessons in Loyalty,* based upon the principles that brought Southwest Airlines such success, she began consulting and speaking on the topic of employee engagement and loyalty, and has worked with many companies to successfully implement programs intended to raise the loyalty of the workforce.

Lorraine welcome to *Roadmap to Success!*

Lorraine Grubbs (Grubbs)

Thank you.

Wright

What makes loyalty more important than ever today?

Grubbs

As we look down the road at the next ten years at the large numbers of people predicted to leave the workforce, and then look at the deficit of available people entering the workforce, the numbers simply don't match. I think this reinforces the importance of creating and maintaining a culture of loyalty; elements vital to businesses today.

Recent numbers indicate that over the next ten years in the United States, there will be about fifty-two million positions that will need to be filled. Thirty-two million of those vacancies will be created by people retiring and leaving the workforce while twenty million new jobs will be created. Of the fifty-two million positions to be filled, we're looking at probably an available employee base of about twenty-three million people to fill them. That leaves a gap of twenty-nine million people! This creates, more than ever before a reason for companies to focus on retaining the talent that they have within their companies.

Additionally, from a competitive perspective, it will be extremely advantageous from a productivity viewpoint for companies to instill a sense of ownership mindset in their employees.

Wright

Does loyalty pay?

Grubbs

Yes. Many successful businesses with loyal workforces have strong statistics that help strengthen their businesses. Look at the results we enjoyed at Southwest Airlines: a turnover of less than 10 percent in an industry with a standard of 26 percent or more. This low turnover was a significant contributing factor in the outstanding return on investment that Southwest Airlines enjoyed over many years. According to *Money* magazine, if you had invested $10,000 in Southwest Airlines stock in the year 1972 it would have been worth over 10.2 million dollars in 2002. Consequentially, there were many millionaires who retired from Southwest Airlines during that time as a result of how well the stock performed. Southwest Airlines was named time and again, within the top ten companies in America to work for. When I was in the People Department, we would receive over 200,000 applications yearly for 3,000 open positions. These are some of the primary reasons that companies such as Southwest Airlines believe loyalty pays.

Wright

Has the definition of loyalty changed in today's environment?

Grubbs

I believe it has. I think in today's environment what companies need to look at is that loyalty isn't necessarily about how long an employee stays with you, but more about what employees do for you while they're with you. Highly engaged employees will be more productive, adopt an ownership mentality, treat your external customers well, and recommend your workplace to their friends and family as a great place to work.

The end result of an employee feeling engaged today is not necessarily about longevity, but about productivity resulting in a better bottom line.

Wright

What is probably the single most important foundational business need for establishing a culture of loyalty?

Grubbs

It has to start from the top. If the leadership at the top does not espouse the value of how important people are to an organization and truly believe and live it (and you can't fake caring about somebody), nothing you put into place will work in the long-term. You can put all the metrics in place that you want, you can put all the programs in place that you want, but it simply won't be sustainable.

As an example, I did a speech in front of a group of people once who were extremely metrics-oriented. At the end of the speech a member of the audience raised his hand and asked me, "How can you measure fun? How do you know when people are having too much fun?" That was an interesting question and it caused me to think that he had probably missed the whole point of having fun in the work environment. Some things should not be measured.

So, to instill the loyalty message in your organization, it's got to start from the top. Leaders in successful organizations know that you've got to have a people-centric leadership philosophy, leaders who "walk their talk" every day with open-door policies, who take the time to get to know employees, and make business decisions taking into account the impact on their people.

One time I was working with a company who asked me to help them establish a culture committee to enhance the culture of their very staid organization. Their leadership was supportive and had given them a budget of $10,000 to start up this committee. I helped them create a plan that included some fun, informal company events.

At the conclusion of the first event I came back and they were so excited. The event had been well attended and everyone had a lot of fun. I asked them how many of their leaders had attended. They said no one had; they were too busy. But, they said, they supported us with the money; wasn't that good enough? I explained that unless the leaders were engaged from the very beginning, unless they show up to the events, unless they fully engaged in the initiative, it was really not going to have the long-term impact that they needed. Sadly, within four or five months, their initiative did indeed fail.

Fully engaged and supportive leadership is the foundation for a successful loyalty culture.

Wright

What role does hiring play in the loyalty of employees?

Grubbs

It's probably the second most important thing. Once the leadership believes, espouses, and lives it, then you've got to find people with the right kind of attitude to bring into your company. Successful companies have defined the values they want represented in their organizations and they hire to those values. For example, if you want people to be loyal, you need to define what you want loyalty to look like in your organization. Is it respect for others, great customer service, empathy, a family environment? In the interview process you need to design the questions around these values in order to solicit the appropriate experience of the applicant. For example, if treating people with respect is one of your core values at XYZ company, then how do you know that the person you're interviewing is going to embrace that value?

You need to identify the behaviors of that dimension (treating people as you want to be treated—putting yourself in others' shoes) and create interview questions such as, "Describe a time when you went above and beyond for a customer without being asked, and what happened?" By identifying and interviewing to the loyalty dimensions you value, you will stand a much better chance of hiring the right individual from the start.

Wright

Reward and recognition are important parts of elevating loyalty. What are companies doing to recognize both excellence in performance and support during tough times in their employees' lives?

Grubbs

A lot of companies know that rewards and recognition are an important strategy of any successful organization when building a loyal culture. Many companies, however, have a haphazard approach to recognition. They have a couple of planned events a year, a few internal programs that they count on their leaders to come up with and implement and that's it.

Successful companies have well-defined processes and strategies for recognition just like other more operational areas of their business. The programs are well documented and ensure someone within the organization owns it. They also pay attention to the timing of the major events to ensure they are occurring throughout the entire year.

A good place for any company to start is by looking inward. What's already happening in your company and how can you build on and formalize existing programs? People have a tendency to do it for themselves in the absence of a structured program. Go to your employee groups and document what they are already doing. Consolidate those ideas into a booklet and give it as a gift to every single new manager who is promoted. Put a metric in place for the leader's performance evaluation to ensure recognition and rewards are a part of his or her measured performance.

Some companies erroneously think that reward and recognition costs a lot of money, therefore they don't do it as much as they should. We didn't have a lot of money at Southwest Airlines. We knew it was not about the big events as much as it was about the little things. It's recognizing and rewarding the things your employees want, taking into account that not everybody's going to value the same thing. Not everybody's going to appreciate going bowling one day as a team-building event, for example.

Get to know your employees, their wants and their needs and then try to reward appropriately. It's the phone call, the card, the pat on the back—those are the things most people will remember.

At one company I worked with, we established a formal "Connections" program whereby the leaders of each department were kept apprised of any life events in their employees' lives, both happy and sad events. It was owned by and run through the administrative assistants throughout the company. As soon as the leader was made aware of the event, a card, e-mail or note would go out to the employee and family. The event was conducted as a contest via the administrative assistants of each department and the assistant whose department had the highest percentage of life event notices were rewarded at the end of the year.

An important thing to remember in recognizing employees is to keep in mind that there are two different types of employees. There are the employees who are in front of the customers and there are the employees who are behind the scenes. What are you doing to ensure both are getting recognized? At Southwest Airlines we had a "Heroes of the Heart" award given to behind-the-scene employees nominated by their peers. It was only available to employees who had no direct external customer interaction in an effort to give them the recognition they deserved.

Have you considered including your customers in the appreciation of your employees? What kinds of programs do you have in place so that the customer is encouraged to write in and recognize someone? Are you sending the kudos letters/cards, etc. to employees' homes so their families can be included in the recognition? Additionally, are you recognizing the families at every single corporate event? Do you have special awards for the families, without whose support you wouldn't be able to have that employee working those fourteen-hour days or whatever it takes to get the projects done?

As indicated above, there are two factors to consider when you are recognizing employees: The first is putting a structure in place to recognize the employees in the workplace during good times and tough times. The second is sharing that recognition with their families. To ensure that your programs are implemented on a consistent basis, create a strategic plan and designate an owner of the process. Measure recognition in leaders' evaluations. As we mentioned above, it doesn't have to be costly. It's the little things that count in employees' lives—the birth of a child, the cards sent for a mother's illness—the critical thing is that someone own the recognition process and that someone is also getting measured on whether it's getting done.

Wright

How many kinds of customers does a company have?

Grubbs

Companies actually have several different customers. The first, and most important to the loyalty concept, is the employee, or the internal customer, which includes the families of employees. Then there is the external customer. The external customers are typically the ones who are going to be buying or utilizing your product. Other external customers include the community in which you do business, governmental agencies that govern your business, vendors, and partners. Again, the more successful companies today recognize that all relationships are important and worth developing. Make them feel like part of your company or family and you will enhance the effectiveness of your business.

In my book, *Lessons in Loyalty,* I talk about how a friend of mine used to be the head of the FAA control tower at Hobby Airport. He told me one day, "I don't know whether you realize this, but Southwest's planes have a higher on-time arrival rate at Hobby Airport than your competitors, in part because your pilots are very respectful of the dispatchers. Instead of demanding an altitude, and speaking down to the dispatchers, they treat them with respect. When requesting something from the dispatchers, they ask in a respectful manner, utilizing simple words like please and thank you. They get to know the dispatcher and that makes all the difference in the world to the relationship. Thus, when traffic hour is high and all planes are trying to get in at the same time, your pilots actually get preferential treatment."

When you develop great relationships with your customers outside of your employees, your customers will help you succeed.

Wright

How does leadership differ in a company with a high loyalty approach?

Grubbs

Typically, the leaders will value their people. As they create and implement business plans, they will take into account the impact on people.

This does not mean that they will ignore the bottom line; a company still has to make money. It's not about putting people first for the sake of valuing them and letting the business lose money. It's about recognizing that if your people feel valued and respected, they will be more productive. Treat your customers better and ultimately produce a better bottom line. Leaders who understand that principle are the ones who realize that when someone gets up in the morning and enjoys going to work they turn the "job" into more of a mission and a cause. Again, as a leader, the important thing to remember is "you can't fake caring." People will see right through that.

I think leaders who are more successful in building loyalty cultures are motivators. They know how to light the fire and turn their employees into "warrior spirits." They are very good communicators and they insist on excellent communication across the organization. These leaders are out among the troops often, walking the talk and ensuring they know what is going on. They have an open door policy, and employees understand that they can get their issues heard and resolved in a timely manner.

Leaders who are not naturally charismatic compensate by surrounding themselves with people who are. At one company I worked with, the company had grown too big for the senior leaders to be out as much as they would have liked, so we created the LIFT (Leaders in the Field Today) program. Each location received a visit from a senior officer and director at least twice a year. The location visits were coordinated through a central department to ensure consistency of messaging, processes, and follow-up.

Wright

What role does communication play in engaging employees?

Grubbs

Behind leadership mindset and hiring the right people, I believe it's the third most important factor in building a loyalty culture. Without good communication, you simply won't earn the trust of your people. In today's hectic world most companies are operating at speeds that feel like 150 miles an hour. Successful companies form very powerful infrastructures for communication. Many companies are decentralized so the need is even greater to ensure the communication gets to the entire workforce.

You simply cannot over communicate. Invest the time to determine what forms of communication are important to your company. For example, I once had a company identify every avenue of communication that existed where they were inviting the employee to submit ideas, questions, or simply communicate what was on their minds. The result was that we discovered the communication infrastructure was broken. Many voicemails were never updated or even checked, e-mail messages not returned, and suggestion boxes never cleared out. As a result, we reinstituted what they already had and ensured someone owned the process so that no matter who was in the position, it became part of their responsibility.

It is as important to communicate the bad news as the good. In fact, employees, like external customers, would rather hear the bad news firsthand than try to second-guess the "why" behind something. Passengers would much rather know why a flight is delayed than to just sit there in silence second-guessing what is going on. Successful companies realize that trust is built by admitting mistakes and saying "I'm sorry." They explain the reason why a decision that went south was made (intent), and what was learned from the mistake.

A good example of this is the $25 fare campaign Southwest Airlines ran during my tenure there. In a strategic move to improve sluggish fourth quarter bookings, a campaign to allow people to fly anywhere that Southwest flew for just $25 was created. For maximum exposure, it was advertised on Monday Night Football. It was so well received by our customers that we immediately became overwhelmed by the numbers of calls. Within hours we had shut down all our reservations phone lines and the phone lines to our headquarters. When people couldn't get through to reservations, they would run to the airport.

We quickly pulled the ad and any mention of the promotion, and for the next few days we dealt with all the demand. It was all hands on deck as our employees stayed late, night after night, accommodating the demand. When the dust settled, our employees were not happy and began questioning the wisdom of the campaign.

Southwest did two things immediately that kept the employee morale on track. They came out with an apology to the employees about the impact to their personal lives, followed by a big thank you to all those frontline employees who were affected by the promotion. Then they explained that the fourth quarter bookings were now solid and as a result, the company expected to make money in a tough quarter, thus translating into more profit sharing for the employees. Once the employees understood the "why" behind the campaign, and were thanked for helping us through it, they immediately settled down and went back to work. The company, however, did promise to think more thoroughly through promotions in the future!

Wright

How do you get employees to feel like owners of the company, thereby embracing the "doing more with less" philosophy?

Grubbs

Again, it starts with hiring people with the right mindset from the onset. One of the values we espoused at Southwest Airlines was keeping costs low. We asked questions to support that value in our interviews. After hiring the right mindset, you must ensure your employees feel like they have a voice in the business and are empowered to make decisions. At Southwest Airlines we were always taught (and experienced) that as long as your intent was to help the customer, we would forgive any mistake.

Employees need to know that if they have ideas, someone will listen. In fact, employee focus groups were a mainstay at Southwest Airlines. Prior to making any major decisions impacting our employees or customers, we would bring in frontline employees and ask for their input.

After 9/11 the boarding process got very laborious and frustrating. Southwest Airlines boards passengers in groups: A, B, and C. There is no assigned seating, so if you wanted the best pick of seats, our customers knew they had to get to the airport early to get that coveted "A" boarding pass so they could board first.

Just after 9/11, the TSA set up secondary screening at the boarding gate and they would randomly select passengers from all boarding groups to be pulled aside and screened. Naturally, if you were one of the passengers selected and you were in the "A" boarding group, by the time the TSA would complete the screening, you found yourself boarding with the "C" group. The effort that they made to get to the airport early was lost and they became angry and upset. Our flight attendants, recognizing what was happening, began reserving the first two rows of each aircraft to mitigate the impact of the secondary screening. They didn't ask permission—they didn't have to even get permission—they just made the decision to do it.

If you have a way to tie performance to profit sharing, you will also find this is a great way to build employee ownership. At Southwest Airlines, all employees, regardless of position, received the same percentage of profit, predicated upon their salary.

Rewarding employees for good ideas keeps your creative culture alive while creating ownership. It doesn't have to be monetary reward, it could tie back to your already established recognition program. Ultimately, you want that employee to think and act and treat your business as theirs. After all, no one treats a business better than the owner of that business.

Help employees understand the finances of the business and what part they play. Communicate that message in simple terms; break it down so they "get it."

Southwest co-founder and Executive Chairman Herb Kelleher, told employees that if they made a point to save the company five dollars per day, by the end of the year, it would impact the bottom line by millions of dollars. We got our groups together and brainstormed how to save five dollars a day. We implemented ideas such as bringing coffee cups from home, collecting pens from the hotels in which we stayed when we traveled, etc.

Owners are created when people feel empowered, when they feel like their ideas are heard, and when someone keeps them in the loop on what is going on. Even if their ideas cannot be implemented, they need to know that someone considered it and gave them feedback on it.

Wright

What a great conversation and a new definition of loyalty. I really enjoyed talking with you and all the time you've spent with me to answer these questions. I really learned a lot and I'm sure our readers will as well.

Grubbs

Well thank you David. I've enjoyed it also.

Wright

Today we've been talking with Lorraine Grubbs. Her recently published book, *Lessons in Loyalty,* outlines the principles utilized by Southwest Airlines to create one of the most productive and successful cultures. Her book is quickly gaining momentum in the business community as a primer for companies who want to know how Southwest Airlines does it.

Lorraine, thank you so much for being with us today on *Roadmap to Success.*

ABOUT THE AUTHOR

Lorraine is the president of *Lessons in Loyalty*; a company specializing in helping organizations create cultures where employees come to work because they want to, not because they have to; recognizing that happy employees create loyal customers. Lorraine's recently published book, *Lessons in Loyalty*, outlines the principles utilized by Southwest Airlines to create one of the most productive and successful cultures, and is quickly gaining momentum in the business community as a primer for companies who want to know how Southwest Airlines does it.

Lorraine has recently completed a two year assignment as the Vice President of People (Human Resources) at Pinnacle Airlines in Memphis, TN where she successfully implemented the lessons of her book in this highly profitable regional air carrier. Prior to Pinnacle, as a 15-year veteran of Southwest Airlines, Lorraine was ultimately the Director of Employment, tasked with "hiring Warrior Spirits". Her track record includes her ability to achieve optimal results in times of chaos, high stress, change and reorganization. She commuted daily to Dallas from her home on a sailboat in Clear Lake, TX. In 1986, Lorraine started her own aviation charter company at Hobby Airport which, within 3 years, boasted billings of over three million dollars.

Lorraine has been a public speaker and consultant for many years, bringing the message of employee engagement and loyalty to businesses throughout the country.

Lorraine speaks three languages and when not speaking or flying, is cruising on her boat and home, Naciente.

Lorraine Grubbs

Lessons in Loyalty
2951 Marina Bay Dr. #130-136
League City, TX 77573
281-813-0305
lgrubbs@lessonsinloyalty.com
www.lessonsinloyalty.com

out

ROADMAP ^{to} SUCCESS 12

An interview with...

Lorin Beller Blake

David Wright (Wright)

Today we're talking with Lorin Beller Blake. She entered the professional world as a spirited entrepreneur in the health and wellness field, working as a stress management and goal setting trainer and counselor. As a business savvy industrialist she successfully co-founded and developed Global 2000, one of the first local Internet service providers in the country. She later sold the company and stayed on in the new company, Business Online, as the Vice-President of Sales and Marketing. While there she played a major role in advancing the company by acquiring and integrating more than thirteen companies in over two years while working on the team to take the entity public.

Lorin Beller Blake is founder of Big Fish Nation, a year long business development program that leads entrepreneurs toward maximizing their lives and business goals using a unique combination of tele-classes and one-on-one coaching delivered by highly trained business coaches. Big Fish Nation and Lorin Beller Blake have been nationally recognized by *Investors Business Daily* and Lorin was named one of the Top 30 Female Executives of 2004 by *Female Entrepreneur Magazine*. She has also been a featured speaker for Sales and Marketing Executive International, the internationally known Young Entrepreneur Organization, and Canada's Women in Business National Expo. She is a co-host on the *Kathryn Zox's Radio Show* on Voice American Weekly, which is currently the most listened to show on the Women's channel.

Lorin, welcome to *Roadmap to Success*.

Lorin Beller Blake (Blake)

Thank you, David.

Wright

So the title of your chapter is "The Zen of Business." I can already see it's going to be a different chapter, so tell our readers what you mean by Zen.

Blake

Well, first let me actually define the word "Zen" from Webster's perspective. Webster says that Zen means: "aims at enlightenment."

Wright

And what do you mean by enlightenment?

Blake

Well, that is another word I looked up in the dictionary because I wanted to be sure that we're speaking from the same dictionary. When we look up the word "enlightenment" Webster's dictionary defines it as, "a blessed state marked by the absence of desire or suffering." I thought that was critical—a very important point in this process. How many people *suffer* through the process of their work? Or are they constantly in a state of wanting more? I think what we're talking about when we talk about the Zen of business is being present to what is. In other words, in our world these days there's so much said about the desire for more, and gathering more things, more items, and more trinkets. In order to get those things we suffer through the process and we make it hard—it's got to be difficult—and remember the old adage, no pain no gain? I lived that way far too long, and this is not what I'm talking about here. Enlightenment is the realization that work can be easy and success does not have to be difficult. It's about finding the beautiful balance between loving and enjoying our work as it is right now and striving toward the goals that we have.

Wright

So what is the Zen of business?

Blake

It's important that we define this early on, so the Zen of business is about building your business while enjoying the process. And said another way or to give it another perspective, to be present with where your business is right now. I know there are so many businesspeople who will be reading this book who are striving and searching for that magic bullet, the magic ingredient, the magic formula. When money's low and debts are high, what we tend to do is to get more stressed and our behavior becomes frantic. What we really need to do is actually just the opposite. If we were truly to listen to our intuition, we will understand that we need to get quiet and look at what truly needs to be done. And then, we need to quietly, yet very assertively, set out and tackle the tasks at hand. We need to breathe and be diligent to that process. More importantly, we need to trust ourselves and trust the business that we've committed ourselves to.

Wright

How as a businessman do I practice Zen—how do I practice it as I conduct my business?

Blake

First I think it's about habits and discipline. When I think about Zen, the image that often comes to mind is a person who is sitting quietly with their palms facing up on their knees in a yoga position. What these people tend to do is practice very basic things over and over, to get excellent at be masters at breathing, relaxing, and at focusing. That is what practicing the Zen of business is all about. It's finding the habits and the discipline that are absolutely critical and beneficial to the bottom line—the positive bottom line of our business. It's about mastery, it's about practice, it's about consistency in behavior, and loving those practices at the same time. I would add to that it's also about taking bold action regularly and consistently.

I think so many times in business, we pay more consistent attention to the minutiae instead of taking consistent bold action. The difference between these two approaches will create very different results. The Zen of business is about finding wild success in routine, yet powerful behaviors that separate wild success from those that are not.

Wright

The way you explained the way most people think of Zen was the exact picture I had in my mind.

Blake

I think that's how most of us think of the word "Zen." I'm glad you said that because this is so not about sitting quietly and just meditating on what we want. Instead it is about wild action, yet very disciplined behavior. So thanks for saying that, because I do think that many people will be seeing that picture in their mind and wonder, "How does that relate to business?"

Wright

Will you give us some real examples of practicing Zen in the business world?

Blake

Yes, let's do that! Scenario one: Money is tight, clients are not keeping us very busy, so what do we tend to do? What I find, is entrepreneurs will often use the help of a coach. When we explore what they are doing with their time, we find that they are doing activities such as: e-mail, cleaning the office, speaking to existing clients, spending time chatting with employees or vendors, organizing the files, etc. I don't mean to indicate that these activities are not important, they are; but in this current situation it will not change the bottom line and bring more customers. So the "Zen" thing to do is just the opposite. We need to: pick up the phone and speak with potential clients, go to meetings with potential client, set up a forum to meet with potential clients, implement our marketing plan. You will see very different results come from the two types of actions.

Let's look at another scenario: You just landed a big contract! Many folks tend to "quit and go celebrate!"—golf, have a drink, go home, etc. No! The Zen approach would be to use that energy to do more of the same. You see, when we land a big contract we have great, high energy; *use it* to create more of the same. Again, these two behaviors will create very different results and an improved bottom line at the end of the day.

Let's look at one more scenario: A new business owner has been in business for herself for over a year and she feels that she can take her business to a whole new level. However, she feels that she does not know the "correct" way to grow the business so she reaches out to a business consultant to "tell her how to grow the business." In this scenario, the owner does not trust herself—the very person who had the vision in the first place. I do think reaching out for help is a great tool, but never lose trust in yourself in the process. Your intuitions really point you in the "right" direction if you would only listen more to yourself and take bold action. I think in business we tend to move too slowly, when we "see what is next for ourselves" the Zen approach is move it—act! Again, this is the opposite of what I often find when working with leaders.

Do those three scenarios help you see what the Zen of business is all about David?

Wright

Yes, for sure, Lorin; and now I am seeing how important the various aspects of Zen are. Will you help us understand better what the role of the mind is in the Zen of business? In the scenarios that you shared, I can see that sometimes our mind might get in the way.

Blake

I think the mind is a critical piece of the Zen of business because it's about attitude. I think that a real story here might highlight the importance of the mind. This particular businesswoman had told herself for years that she wanted more work. Over the years of working through a coaching program, she realized that "more work" was not what she wanted. What she really wanted was a better bottom line and to be more productive. She was being very effective in getting exactly what she wanted, so it was time to change the game. She changed her thinking and she worked on her company's policies, procedures, and processes. Through applying the new thought process and her new attitude to her work, she actually increased her bottom line over 300 percent over the course of twelve months!

First of all, the role of the mind is about attitude—what attitudes you bring to the table each day and what attitudes you bring to your tasks each day. I do believe that if we bring a positive attitude to the same tasks, we would see good results. If two people have the same task, one with a positive attitude and one with the negative attitude, we're going to get very different results. That's the role of the mind.

The other role of the mind is how present we are able to be in each moment. Some people go through the motions of a task but are not present in it. Other people go through a task and enjoy every moment of it. These two different approaches will create very different results. This is why the old adage, "Do what you love and the money will follow" has value.

Wright

Speaking of doing what you love, we've talked about the mind, what is the role of the heart in the Zen of business?

Blake

It has everything to do with business. If you look at people who are wildly successful, they love what they do. We do need to ask ourselves: Do we love what we're doing? Are we passionate about our results, our service, and the product that we're putting out into the world? Do we see what we're putting out into the world as having impact and value, and are we feeling good about implementing it?

I spoke to a woman recently who was in the dog food business. She was very excited about her business. I asked her what her goal was in speaking with me. She said her goal this year was to double her business (she already had a significant business). As I was listening to her, her enthusiasm, her love for what she was doing, her excitement, her vision, and just as important, her plan for doubling her business, I knew that there was nothing that was going to get in her way of that goal. She could see what was possible and she had a plan to make it a reality. She was providing all natural dog food, delivered to the customer's doorstep. It was easy, it was affordable—a no brainer during this time of the necessity of finding quality food options for dog owners! It was easy for her to double her income because she loved the process. She would wake up every day with another brilliant idea, and another brilliant partnership, and another brilliant way to promote and advertise her business. It was happening almost without thought—one thing kept leading to the next magical idea, and the next magical action. It was such a great example of one's heart being in one's business. The last time I spoke with her she was actually close to meeting her financial goals.

What does heart have to do with business? Everything! Our heart needs to be in our business 100 percent. When we lose our passion, it is hard to find it again. When our heart is in the business, it keeps us in the game and that consistency—that "stick-to-itiveness"—is the difference between wild success and failure.

The other thing that having our heart in our business means is that it allows us to listen better to our own intuition. If we can "hear" what is "right" for our business we will tend to take wild, bold action because there is a knowledge about that action versus feeling that we are guessing or second-guessing the next steps.

Wright

One of the things that separates the great from the not so great is vision. I wonder why vision is so important and how will I know if I can achieve my vision—how does vision inform us today?

Blake

Vision—as with heart—goes hand-in-hand. When we have our heart in our business with us, it helps us see what kind of impact our service and/or product can have when put into the world. So, vision is absolutely a critical component to achieve success for many, many reasons. It gives us a destination. And how many times have we become tired, how many times have we gotten frustrated, and how many times have we become lost? If we have this tool called vision and it's documented, very clear, and used regularly, it's a great reminder of why we're doing what we're doing every day.

I have all the people I work with write down their ten-year vision. People will often think, "Well, what kind of business tool is this?" My answer is that it is the most critical business tool there is. It is the tool that gets people back on track, gets them out of the maze of minutiae, and informs them about how they should be working today.

Wright

What are Zen business tools that I can apply to by business?

Blake

Great question, David. Let's get practical with this thing called a Zen approach to business!

The first tool is to *have a vision.* The people who have vision often think it as something for tomorrow. But that is not really the full picture. The goal is that the vision informs us exactly how and what we should be working on today! That is the power of a really powerful vision. If it does not do that, it is not a strong enough vision.

The second tool is to *have a written plan*—a business plan—on how we are going to get to that vision. This should be very simple. For years I followed the Franklin Covey goal-setting system, where you set goals, you set a process in place—very important steps. These steps made me think about how I get from A to B. It's that Zen breath-work. It's that step one, step two, step three, and let's go do it again. It's actually repeating the same process and setting a lot of the same goals. It helps to increase our sales, it helps to increase our networking, and it's the marketing. For every aspect of business there are basic processes that need to be done over, and over. We think that doing things over and over isn't going to get us anywhere, but as long as those processes are working, documented, and have consistent impact, we should continue doing them. Does that make sense?

Wright

Absolutely. What is the role of traditional sales and marketing using the Zen approach to business?

Blake

This is interesting because I think that often, people hope that when they come to a business they won't have to do sales. They think they can just meditate on business coming in the door, we need to "see it in our minds eye for sure," but that is not the only tool here—we actually have to "do business" too. So let's talk about more of those practical tools.

The third tool is to *have a sales process documented.*

The process of traditional sales is really appropriate and needed in every business. What is different, however, in the sales process in the Zen approach to business is asking the question: is the sales process authentic or not? In other words, do we really care about whether or not our product/service will have a positive impact on the people who purchase it? If we can honestly say yes to that question, then our sales process is authentic and having that sales process is a good thing! Most of us stop short in the sales process and never complete the sale out of fear of something. If the process is documented and you take every person through all the steps, you will increase your bottom line!

The fourth practical tool is to *have a written marketing plan.*

Marketing—introducing people to your product or service—is a process that needs to be done over and over again in any business. Business is just a cycle and marketing is part of the beginning of that cycle. I like to introduce people to a simple marketing planning process that has them consistently in action with various forms of introducing people to their business; but the key here is *consistency*. This is very Zen as well. Again, it is that "practice" of the basics over and over again, whether it is weekly or monthly. Consistently introducing new people to your business is important. This is the only way we can have consistent sales and new people/customers.

Wright

Every time you say the word "Zen" I have these images come to mind of a teacher or a master, so how do I learn the Zen of business? Who is the teacher, who's the master, and where do I go for support?

Blake

Well, that's a great question, and there are so many teachers out there. Over the years I think we've had a number of spiritual Zen masters in the world. The "master," however, is not any one person. Each of us has different things to learn about success, business, and the personal growth that goes along with these elements.

I have had many teachers over the years: Stephen Covey, Wayne Dyer—there are so many great teachers out there. No one person is "the" teacher. But the Zen approach here is that we see many as our teachers. Some teach us by more of how we want to be and others teach us more of how we do not want to be—both are teachers. Recently, there has been a lot of talk about the law of attraction, and yes, those people are teachers too. Just as importantly, I think that this process is about our finally listening to ourselves as the Master.

And at the same time, I think it's important to have support. In this day and age, coaching is booming and I do feel very strongly that people should have coaches through this process of striving for success. As they listen to themselves they tend to back off in action, so I think it is critical to have a quality coach to support them so that when they say yes to something they will follow through with it.

Wright

So who has the map on the pathway to success—what's the compass, the vehicle, and the fuel?

Blake

Success is literally a journey. No one can tell you exactly what success means for you or how your journey should go. We need to define success so we're not chasing it. We need to define very clearly for ourselves what success is, and to be sure each day that we are taking action and doing active things to move us forward toward our own success.

A mistake that is often made is that we never stop to notice that we are successful already! We just keep chasing what we think is success. So from a Zen approach, it is an important step to stop and notice where we are already successful. This step will cause us to see ourselves as a success now and this, in and of itself, is very powerful.

You also asked about the fuel. To answer that question, let's ask a question: If our vehicle broke down on the side of the road, how long would we work on that vehicle ourselves before we'd ask for help? For me, it would be about one minute because I do not know about vehicles and engines and I am very aware of that fact. We need to be sure that our vehicle is constantly moving forward. The fuel is *action*—forward action. What I know of people— business people—is that when we take action it begets more action—action creates action. The fuel is action. If people feel stuck, the first thing is to get them moving; after that they'll find the next step, but to stay in action is the fuel.

Wright

I'm pretty close to getting what you're saying. I've never thought the words "Zen" and "business" in the same sentence in my entire life. So how do I stay on the path, what do I do when I get lost, and what about the detours? I've had plenty of those.

Blake

We all have! Detours are part of the journey.

I was fortunate enough a couple weeks ago, to have what our family now calls our Christmas 2007 adventure. It was the Friday before Christmas; we had no company coming for the holiday and we wanted an adventure. At the very last minute we decided that we wanted to see snow for Christmas. We currently live in Austin, Texas—no chance of snow. So we packed up our car in about an hour including our suitcases and our two-year-old daughter and our dog! We knew our destination—Santa Fe, New Mexico. We set out at

5:00 PM Christmas weekend for an eleven-hour drive one way. It was a total adventure. How did we get there? We just kept moving. We had to remember our vision, we had to remember what we were trying to go, and the reason we decided to take the journey in the first place. Part of the journey included getting lost; part of the journey was to see the sights along the way. Part of it was unknown, such as where we would sleep that night; and definitely part of it was the anticipation of snow at the end at some point.

So, I think detours are totally fine along the way, as long as we're *conscious* that they're detours. Again, that is a real Zen word. Are we being conscious of the fact that we are on a detour? When we are not conscious about it and lose sight of our destination we get ourselves into trouble. What we want to be conscious of is that we're saying yes to our detours, and that's a very important Zen point.

Wright

How do I know when I've arrived at success?

Blake

As I said before, success is a journey, not a destination. I also believe that success is a feeling, not a destination. Once we "get there" I think that we, as normal businesspeople, see the next place to go, which always fun. I help people find that feeling of success. This is important—identifying what success feels like. In essence, from a Zen approach, we bring success in rather than chase it. The goal for me as a business coach is help people feel like they have arrived at success rather than have people chase it. Working from this new "arrived" place creates very different results too—again that's a very Zen approach to the process of success

Wright

So what is the role of gratitude in the Zen approach to business?

Blake

To me, this is a really important question; it tends to be like a left turn and it's really not. In my opinion, gratitude is just as critical as vision. It is another practical business tool.

It's one of those business components that I find in seasoned businesspeople. Gratitude is a key ingredient early on, not when they get there. In other words, being grateful and being able to be in gratitude early on in business is a critical element versus waiting until we've arrived at success to be grateful. I teach people to look immediately for all the things they are already grateful for and acknowledge these things both to themselves and to others. This process naturally moves them toward their success more quickly and brings their success to them more quickly. Telling people face-to-face how much you appreciate them and their contribution to your business encourages them to continue to want to do a great job whether they are employees, vendors, or even customers. This acknowledgement steps up the function of any business.

I know that every single one of us has at least one thing to be grateful about today. If I work with someone long enough we can find at least ten things. Being grateful is the entrance gate to success, not the exit gate. You can see how gratitude helps success come full circle.

Wright

What a great conversation. I have really learned a lot today. I've not only learned but I've decided to start looking at things a little bit differently now and I have you to thank for that. I really appreciate all the time you've taken with me here to answer these questions.

Blake

My pleasure. I hope we continue to inspire others to start thinking of business and success as a more relaxed and fun way to approach this thing that we often make hard.

Wright

Today we've speaking with Lorin Beller Blake, founder of Big Fish Nation, a year long business development program that leads entrepreneurs toward maximizing their lives and business goals. Just as many of the Big Fish she works with, Lorin was ready to stop working for someone else and make life work for her. She left the corporate world to pursue her dream of coaching fellow entrepreneurs toward redefining their vision so they to could make a big splash in their lives and business. She formed Big Fish Nation in 2004 and since then she has been fulfilling her dream—sharing her Big Fish principles with thousands of entrepreneurs nationwide through her innovative program, which has been promoted nationally as a Zen approach to business.

Lorin, thank you so much for being with us today on *Roadmap to Success*.

Blake

Thank you, David.

About the Author

Lorin Beller Blake is the founder of Big Fish Nation, a year long business development program that leads entrepreneurs toward maximizing their lives and business goals. Just as many of the Big Fish she works with, Lorin was ready to stop working for someone else and make life work for her. She left the corporate world to pursue her dream of coaching fellow entrepreneurs toward redefining their vision so they to could make a big splash in their lives and business. She formed Big Fish Nation in 2004 and since then she has been fulfilling her dream—sharing her Big Fish principles with thousands of entrepreneurs nationwide through her innovative program, which has been promoted nationally as a Zen approach to business.

Lorin Beller Blake
Big Fish Nation
Austin, TX
512.266.2196
Lorin@bigfishnation.com
www.bigfishnation.com

ROADMAP to SUCCESS 13

An interview with...

Susan Steinbrecher

David Wright (Wright)

Today we're talking with Susan Steinbrecher. Susan is an internationally acclaimed businesswoman, executive coach, speaker, and co-author of *Heart Centered Leadership: An Invitation to Lead from the Inside Out*, published by Black Pants Publishing, December of 2003. She is the President and Chief Executive Officer of Steinbrecher and Associates, Inc. founded in 1992, a leadership development consulting firm that provides professional development services in the areas of executive coaching, training, organizational consulting, and group facilitation. She works with leaders and their organizations to develop and implement innovative, life-changing, and profit-building solutions to address global and day-to-day challenges of leadership, operations, and human resources. Steinbrecher and Associates has positively impacted many Fortune 500 and Fortune 100 companies worldwide. She shares her message and philosophies with millions of individuals each year through keynote speaking, radio seminar telecasts, tele-classes, seminars, books, and DVDs.

Susan has been featured in *Chain Leaders* magazine, *Nation's Restaurant News, Restaurants and Institutions Magazine, Private Clubs Magazine,* and *Living Magazine* as well as in numerous articles and interviews. Susan earned her bachelor's degree in Applied Arts and Sciences from Texas State University and an honorary doctorate in Hospitality Management. She holds professional certifications as master practitioner of neurolinguistic programming; she is a certified mediator and a licensed HeartMath coach. Susan is also a member and past president of numerous organizations, and for four consecutive years she received the Business Leadership Center's Teaching Excellence Award at the SMU Cox School of Business.

Susan, welcome to *Roadmap to Success.*

Susan Steinbrecher (Steinbrecher)

Well, thank you so much; it's such pleasure to be with you here today.

Wright

So you have experienced working with successful leaders; what advice do you have for individuals who want to have success in their business?

Steinbrecher

Well, there are certainly a lot of factors that contribute to business success. I've had the opportunity to work with hundreds of leaders and I have noted that the most successful ones seem to possess five core fundamentals and do so at an exceptional level. Those five are:

An unwavering belief that a high level of success is possible,

Courage to step up, take initiative, and act,

Outstanding communication skills

Being able to effectively deal with adversity

Excellent planning or implementation skills

These are the five that I've seen rise to the surface when you look at the common denominator of highly successful people.

Wright

So the first core fundamental that you stated was an unwavering belief that a high level of success is possible. I'm a bit surprised by this—I would have thought that this would be a given.

Steinbrecher

Well, you're right, it sounds like it would be a given and actually it's a simple concept, but not necessarily easy. What I mean is it's having a deep down belief that no matter what, you can be successful. It's an unwavering or unyielding confidence that no matter where you are or what has happened to you in your past, anything is possible. Those who struggle with success are often doing so because they're straddling a fence. They have one foot on the side of possibility and the other foot on the side of "I'm not good enough," or, "It's not possible for me to succeed." So they can't make any movement forward, there's no momentum.

Let me give you an example. I was hired to coach a leader in an organization who by all accounts was successful, but he felt like he was hitting a wall in getting to the next level. What I noticed when I worked with him was that he was reading some great books on leadership, he attended some excellent workshops, he even had a mentor who was willing to help him in any way. But what I noticed was that he wasn't putting any of this information or advice into practice. So that begs the question, if he had been given all of those gifts and tools, why wasn't he able to put what he was learning into practice? The problem was his belief about success. What I was able to uncover was that deep down inside he didn't believe he could have the level of success that he said he wanted.

All the resources in the world can be there for you—the best books, and seminars, and you can get all the best advice—but all is for naught if you're not able to believe that real success is even possible for you. You see, everything starts with a thought. Thoughts repeated over time become beliefs. We operate our lives from our beliefs. This is why I say that having the belief that you can have success is the most critical first step.

Wright

I have heard it stated that seeing is not necessarily believing; so how does someone come to believe that he or she can have success?

Steinbrecher

First and foremost you have to acknowledge that your current level of success has a lot to do with your belief about success. This is difficult because it takes a lot of courage to look in the mirror and own up to your limiting belief about success.

We have the tendency to look outward instead of inward—we will look to others as the reason for our lack of success: "I can't get good employees anymore" or "I don't have the time" or "My significant others in my life aren't going to support me." Certainly these factors may exist but we so often use them as our reasons for not getting what we say we want. The problem with focusing on external factors is that none of this is within our control. People are sabotaging their success unknowingly by putting their focus on external factors instead of looking within.

Once we can acknowledge that there's something going on within us that is causing that lack of success, then we begin to identify ways to work through it so that we can ultimately change our beliefs about success.

Wright

So let's say that someone can acknowledge that he or she has a limiting belief about success. What can the person do about it?

Steinbrecher

Once the limiting belief is identified and the person acknowledges that it is getting in his or her way of achieving full success, we reframe that belief to a new one that serves the person better; then we'll have an action plan designed around that. There is a specific process that we use to do this. We actually come up with action steps the client can take that get him or her to shift from the old belief to the new more empowering belief about success.

Wright

Will you give our readers an example of a client you have worked with who had limiting beliefs that he or she was able to change?

Steinbrecher

Sure. There are numerous clients I could draw upon, but one who always seems to rise to the surface for me is a particular gentleman who contacted me to work with him. He felt he was having some success in his life, but he felt that there was more opportunity for him.

One of the things that struck me when I first started to look at his background information was the fact that he had several advanced degrees. It's interesting for someone to have one, but to have four or five advanced degrees, that's a lot of education; that's striking in and of itself. What was more striking were the kinds of degrees he had earned. They were degrees in nuclear physics and biochemistry. These are challenging degrees, but what was even more striking is what his occupation was—he was a chef! You look at that and wonder why—the degrees he had earned were not even degrees that would help him in his career!

What he was able to discover through my limiting belief process is that he had a belief deep down inside—it was not fully conscious to him—that told him he was stupid. Now the reality is that he was not stupid, but he believed it was the truth, so he spent his whole life trying to get smarter and smarter. He didn't understand that this belief was causing his behavior. He only knew that he had a thirst for knowledge.

The process we use is to first recognize that you've got some beliefs about success. Secondly, if your belief is a limiting one, then you have to move through that, honoring where it has served you and how it has held you back. Third, you have to reframe that old belief into a new one. Your history is your history—it's not what it is today—and today you can choose to move beyond one that does not serve you well. And lastly, create an action plan that identifies ways that you can live with this new reframed belief about success.

Wright

So having the belief that one can have success is your first core fundamental. The second one that you mentioned is having the courage to take initiative, step up, and act. Would you tell us more about this?

Steinbrecher

Yes, as difficult as it can be to do this, the reality is that there's no way you can achieve anything if you're not willing to take some risk—to stretch out there a little bit. I'm not talking about throwing yourself off the cliff, I am talking about calculated risk. Think through the pros and cons of a situation or a decision. Talk with knowledgeable people who can offer suggestions or advice; but once you've done this you must act!

Wright

So why do you think people don't act or take risks?

Steinbrecher

There are a number of reasons, but I have found that with most of the clients I've worked with over the years it's the fear of failure. At the end of the day, it's fear of failure and of course their belief about success that we've already talked about.

Reflecting on my career prior to starting my company, I held the position of a General Manager of a hotel at the very young age of twenty-five. I had a manager who taught me probably one of the most valuable lessons I've ever learned in leadership: before making a decision, ask myself what is the worst thing that can happen? Put the situation in perspective and if you can answer that question and live with the answer, you will have the freedom to risk more. Since learning that valuable lesson, I actually like to look at this question a little bit differently today. I ask: what's the best thing that could possibly happen if I do this? In other words, what is the possibility, what could this decision really create for me if I did it? I think the irony of having a fear of failure is that you are automatically setting up a potential to fail because you're not acting, you're immobile. You're back to straddling the fence again because there's no movement toward anything.

How many organizations have we seen fail because they did not change with the times or they ignored consumer feedback, resting on the successes of their past? I've even seen leaders in organizations get defensive when customers or employees try to provide them very helpful feedback. They don't acknowledge feedback as a gift; they'll get defensive or ignore the information that's actually given to them on a silver platter for free. Organizations that are successful are the ones that have their fingers on the pulse of the consumer or that are in touch with the trends. They openly listen to feedback from their customers and employees. Once that is done, they have to step up and take some calculated risk and act.

Wright

So we've talked about the belief that you can have success and the courage to act and take some risk. The third core fundamental you mentioned is having outstanding communication skills. What in your mind are outstanding communication skills?

Steinbrecher

Communication skills are obviously among the attributes everyone says they want to improve and rightfully so. What I'm referring to here is communication in multiple ways. Talking with someone one-on-one or speaking in a group or communication through e-mails, no matter the vehicle, people must understand that they say so much more with body language and tone of voice than words can ever express.

Several studies have indicated that when we are communicating with somebody, 55 percent of that message being transferred is done so via body language alone, 38 percent by tone of voice, and only 7 percent verbally. That's a lot—93 percent of our message is coming across in ways other than what we say. People often say that can't be possible, but when you really think about it, it makes sense.

All of us have experienced a time when someone has said something to us but we just got the feeling that what was said was not really what was meant. This is what I call an incongruent message—the words say one thing, but the feelings that you're getting from how the person is communicating is sometimes completely different. So now you're in a position where you have to choose which one is the truth—what you just heard or the feeling you're getting? Most people state they believe the feeling they're getting and not the words they heard. You see, we are designed to sense the truth. In most cases, the body can't lie—physiology cannot lie—therefore the true message is the one we're picking up from this person. It's wise to be mindful that we communicate our truth in so many ways that we're not aware of, and it all starts with a thought. So how you think about this person leads to how you feel about this person, which leads to your actions—spoken and unspoken.

The other thing I'm seeing in business today, whether it's one-on-one communication or through e-mails, is that we're not communicating respectfully—we're not paying attention to how we're coming across to somebody. You can have the best technical or tactical management skills in the world, but you're going to fail in your career if you don't have good interpersonal skills. Seventy percent of leaders who fail do so due to lack of interpersonal skills, and this is demonstrated in their communication whether that be one-on-one, small group, or e-mails.

Wright

So you're saying that communication through e-mail is a safe way to go?

Steinbrecher

No, not necessarily. Communicating through e-mails has become the preferred choice, and there are pros and cons to using e-mail.

One leader comes to mind, whose biggest challenge was communication with his team. When I interviewed his team, the common feedback I got from them was that he was very curt, rude, and disrespectful to them, particularly when he communicated in e-mail format. When I brought this to his attention, he didn't understand this feedback. I asked him to send me about twenty e-mails that he had sent to his team members (with the understanding of course that it would be held under the strictest of confidence). I simply wanted to see how he communicated in an e-mail format.

He did send the e-mails and when I reviewed them with him, he was able to see how he had been terse in his correspondence. It is important to note that he was not coming from a negative intention; but simply as a way to save time, he would answer questions with one- or two-word responses. These short responses created a tone other than his intentions. The impact was that his team perceived him to be rude and disrespectful toward them. He often signed his name at the end of the e-mail with just the letter B, instead of his full name. Again, his intention was to save time, but his team interpreted this as arrogance. The net result was a number of strained relationships. In his effort to save time, it cost him more time because he had to take the time to rebuild these relationships.

So no matter what the venue of communication you choose, be mindful of the impact of your thoughts about people. Treat people with respect, fully engage them. In fact, we speak a lot about that in my book, *Heat Centered Leadership*.

Wright

The next core fundamental that you spoke of is dealing effectively with adversity. Of course this is certainly important for people's success. Why do you think it's important?

Steinbrecher

I guess, as I mentioned before, I've had the great fortune to work with a number of very successful leaders. What strikes me is the resiliency these leaders have. In some cases, after hearing about their backgrounds and history, I don't know how they survived it. The common denominator of these leaders centers on adversity—no matter what they are put up against, they're going to find a way to be successful. When things don't go well they don't give up and they don't feel down for long. They choose to pull themselves up; they know they're always on stage. In my book, *Heart Centered Leadership*, we call that, "Know your Impact." They'll rally their team and show their team hope. Collectively they're going to find a solution, and because they have core fundamental number one—belief in success—they undoubtedly do.

Your team observes how you handle adversity. Are you a leader who rises to the occasion and looks for solutions, or one who complains about the situation? Your team observes your behavior and actions and, like it or not, they make decisions about you.

Wright

Can you think of a situation where a leader demonstrated this core value?

Steinbrecher

There are a number of examples that I can share but I'll share a personal story. When I was first promoted into a general manager position, it was during a time when the hotel that I managed had taken a sudden drop in revenue due to numerous market factors.

The timing could not have been worse for me as a leader. It was time for the annual holiday party for employees. I found myself assessing our profit and loss statement, determining quickly that we had no money in the budget for the lavish parties that we had always had in the past. I was so disappointed. I realized that it was not my employees' fault that we were in this situation, yet I felt I needed to continually squeeze every dollar that I possibly could so I could salvage the year. After some soul-searching, I was determined to offer something because those employees really deserved it; but it forced me to be creative. I began to think about what I could do, versus focusing on what I couldn't do.

I came up with an idea of giving the employees in each department of the hotel a $100 dollar budget to work with. I informed them that this year I wanted to approach the holiday party in a more creative way while showcasing their talent at the same time. A lead person in each department received the $100 and in a collaborative manner each department's team created a food theme concept. They were given a six-foot table that they could decorate and provide whatever food they wanted as it related to their theme. For example, the housekeeping department came up with a Mexican food theme. They brought flower arrangements and props from home and each of them took money from this budget and bought the food necessary for some recipes. They prepared the food and brought it to work to place on their tables.

The engineering department selected an Italian food theme since the chief engineer was Italian. They actually built some walls to surround their six-foot table, and hung strands of garlic to decorate their space. Each of the other departments selected their food theme and decorated their tables as well. The result was truly extraordinary! They had a blast being creative and they loved having the opportunity to show off a favorite recipe.

Everyone got into the spirit and the food was exceptional. By far everyone agreed that this was the best holiday party we had ever held. We even invited long-term guests to come to our party and select the top three tables. We awarded prizes for their creativity and effort.

I learned a very valuable lesson through this experience—if you believe there is a way, there is! And don't let potential obstacles like budget get in your way of doing what is right. The truth is that because of tough economic times I was forced to think about alternative ways—to look at what is possible and to think outside the box for solutions.

Wright

Your last core fundamental was excellent planning and implementation skills. Would you tell our readers why this is so important?

Steinbrecher

You can have the best creative vision or the best ideas, and it goes absolutely nowhere if you don't know how to take that idea or vision and implement it. This is where the real work is. It takes a sense of discipline to see something through. When you think about it, name any goal that you've ever achieved, whether it's personal or professional, and you'll realize that it's achieved by taking action. It's achieved by a series of steps that take you from the vision to completion of the goal. Ask yourself, "What are the milestones I need to reach to complete this goal?" If you don't identify the milestones, then the goal feels overwhelming and unachievable. Then one doesn't move at all, therefore the vision or idea is lost.

I watched a woman being interviewed on television about the fact that she had lost 100 pounds and has successfully kept if off for over a year. When asked how she achieved this level of success without surgery or drugs she said that one day it clicked with her. The reason she was not able to lose weight was because she knew that she needed to lose over one hundred pounds; the thought of that was overwhelming to her. She decided to set her sights on a smaller goal and then go from there. So she set her milestone goal to lose twenty pounds. When she achieved that she set her next milestone goal for another twenty pounds. Eventually she did lose the one hundred pounds. This is an excellent example of how to achieve the big picture goals or the vision—

by setting and accepting a step at a time and celebrating success along the way she was able to tackle what felt like an overwhelming goal.

Wright

So we've covered all the core fundamentals that you feel are important to success. Is there anything else you would like to leave our readers with?

Steinbrecher

A practice that I highly recommend is expressing gratitude for all that we have in our lives. Being sincerely, and authentically grateful for friends or family or employees or customers, our home, health, etc. We often take these for granted and assume that they'll always be there. Who is in your life right now that if removed would substantially change your life? Does this person know that? Does the person know the value that he or she holds with you? How have you shown this person the value that you have for him or her?

Expressing gratitude can change your life. One of the things I often see is a lack of gratitude expressed with leaders about their employees.

Wright

So how does expressing gratitude translate at work?

Steinbrecher

Quite honestly, employees have so many choices today; they don't have to work for you. We speak about this is our book, *Heart Centered Leadership,* as well. Knowing that associates have a choice, what are we doing to make sure that our employees are giving 100 percent of their talent to us? It starts with having the gratitude that these employees choose to work with you and choose to work with your organization. It's not taking them for granted and it's about treating them with respect. There are numerous research studies out there telling us that a lack of appreciation or respect or recognition are some of the top reasons that employees choose to quit a job. We also know by our research that people don't typically quit an organization, they really quit their boss. Turnover is extremely expensive for businesses so it really warrants some further review. I do think that it does start with the leader expressing gratitude for his or her employees. With this mindset I think the other things come naturally.

Wright

Well, what a great conversation. I've really learned a lot. Today we've been talking with Susan Steinbrecher, an internationally acclaimed businesswoman, an executive coach, a speaker, and co-author of *Heart Centered Leadership: An Invitation to Lead from the Inside Out.* She works with leaders in their organizations to develop and implement innovative life-changing and profit-building solutions to address global and day-to-day challenges of leadership operations and human resources.

Susan, thank you so much for being with us today on *Road Map to Success.*

Steinbrecher

Oh you're quite welcome. Thank you for the opportunity and privilege to speak with you today.

ABOUT THE AUTHOR

Susan Steinbrecher, an internationally acclaimed businesswoman, executive coach, speaker, and author, is president and CEO of Steinbrecher and Associates, Inc., a management-consulting firm that provides professional development services in the areas of executive coaching, group facilitation, and leadership training.

Susan works with senior executives and their organizations to develop and implement innovative, life-changing, and profit-building solutions to address the global and day-to-day challenges of leadership, operations, human resources, and training.

Susan's expertise has positively impacted companies worldwide like Bank of America, Diageo, Capital One, CVS/Caremark, Brinker International, Gaylord Entertainment, Hilton, Miraval Spa and Resorts, Seneca Casino, and Northwest Airlines to name a few.

Susan earned her bachelor's degree in Applied Arts and Sciences from Southwest Texas State University, and an Honorary Doctorate in Hospitality Management. She holds professional certifications as a master practitioner of neuro-linguistic programming, and she is a Certified Mediator and is certified in the Myers-Briggs Type Indicator. She is also a certified HeartMath coach. Her first book, *Heart-Centered Leadership: An Invitation to Lead from the Inside Out* was published in 2004.

Susan is a member of the International Coach Federation, Women's Foodservice Forum, HRPS, and the Council of Hotel and Restaurant Trainers, in which she was past president. For four consecutive years, she has received the Business Leadership Center's Teaching Excellence Award at the SMU Cox School of Business.

Susan Steinbrecher
609 W. Harwood Rd.
Hurst, TX 76054
817.268.3650
info@steinbrecherassociates.com
www.steinbrecherassociates.com
www.instituteofhcl.com

ROADMAP
SUCCESS
14

An interview with...

Monte Wyatt

David Wright (Wright)

Today we are talking with Monte Wyatt, an individual with tremendous leadership and personal development experience. As a Platinum Master Coach and owner of an ActionCOACH Business Coaching practice, Monte helps business owners bring clarity to how they run and manage their business. He considers himself a business generalist by helping business owners in the following areas: sales and marketing, hiring and training, financial controls, leadership, and business productivity. Through the coaching process, he helps his clients as they implement changes and holds them accountable to the improvements and goals they set.

Today Monte is going to introduce us to a concept called "Moments of Truth."

Monte, welcome to *Roadmap to Success*.

Monte Wyatt (Wyatt)

Thank you very much for having me.

Wright

So tell us about business coaching and how you became a business coach.

Wyatt

Business coaching has gained tremendous popularity in the last couple of decades with every size and type of business, due to increased competition, market place challenges, and new opportunities in the world. As your business coach, I provide an outsider's perspective on your business and help you see opportunities that you may be unable to see because of how close you are to the business.

There are four fundamentals to coaching: awareness, education, implementation, and accountability. Awareness helps you identify your opportunities and your barriers. Next, I teach you proven business strategies and tactics to maximize your situation. Then we implement those strategies by identifying who will do what, by when, and how we will make it happen. Lastly, I hold you accountable to making the changes according to the timeline we created.

In addition to these four fundamentals, I have also found how important a business owner's mindset is to the success of his or her business. In most cases, a change in mindset produces a change in the business. Part of my responsibility as a coach is to challenge the owner on any beliefs that may be hindering the business's growth. Oftentimes an improved mindset will produce new sales results, increased profitability, changes in hiring procedures, and better teamwork. So that's a little bit about business coaching and the tremendous impact it can have on your business. Again, I can't stress enough how changing your mindset can change your business.

As far as my background, I spent fourteen years in corporate America with positions in sales, sales training, sales management, and marketing management. However, 80 percent of my time was spent traveling the United

States by plane. When my wife and I began our family, we both wanted a career that would allow me to be home more often. I wanted the opportunity to be a great father and see our kids grow up.

We began looking at other career opportunities and through our research we found ActionCOACH Business Coaching. During the due diligence process, we discovered how my career experience could really help others achieve more in their business. I believe those fourteen years prepared me to coach business owners in their quest for success.

In a matter of a few days, I resigned from my corporate job and became an owner of an ActionCOACH Business Coaching practice. I was excited to begin the journey.

Wright

Let's get started talking about your concept of "Moments of Truth." What do you mean by "Moments of Truth"?

Wyatt

To me Moments of Truth are moments in business, relationships, or life in general when it is really important to leave a great impression. It has to do with the service you provide your customers as well as the character of the owner and the team.

Did you know that the number one reason a customer leaves a business is because of perceived indifference? This means that the customer did not see any difference between you and your competition or any difference in not using the product or service at all. I believe that leaving a good impression should be the goal of every interaction you have with other people, whether it be prospects, customers, clients, or vendors.

In order to leave this level of impression, we have to go back to our discussion on mindset. What you think or believe about yourself, your business, or your team will greatly affect how you behave. Once you have the right beliefs, you need to support those beliefs with the right actions, which may include exceeding others' expectations, being on time both to appointments or deadlines, or recognizing the tone you use when you talk with customers. I once had a person tell me that having this type of mindset would produce a lot of pressure. That was their belief and until that belief changes, it will be hard for them to provide consistent Moments of Truth.

Wright

So why do you believe Moments of Truth are important?

Wyatt

Moments of Truth are important because I believe your mindset will draw people to you and your business. By creating this mindset in yourself, your team, and your business, you will start to consistently provide a high level of service. This service will create return customers, referrals, and lifelong clients. What a great way to grow your business by treating people well and creating a demand of people wanting to do business with you.

Wright

So I think I'm beginning to get it, but would you share a personal example of a Moment of Truth with us?

Wyatt

The example I want to share comes from my own business. Every interaction that I have, whether it's answering a phone call, making a phone call, sending an e-mail, a face-to-face interaction, or conducting a seminar or workshop, I focus on leaving an incredible impression. I do this by being prepared, organized, and by having the confidence that I am providing exactly what my client needs at that point in time. I am also conscious of being professional in both my tone and demeanor. My goal is to provide more than what my prospect or client expects.

For example, if I set an appointment with you today for the end of next week, I am going to interact with you three or four times before that appointment. The first interaction is today's phone call. The second may be an informational packet that you receive in the mail. The third interaction is a follow-up call to ensure you received the packet, and the fourth may be a fax or an e-mail somewhere in the middle. By making each of these contacts (or following my touch point strategy), my goal is to begin to create a relationship by making "deposits" into your "emotional bank account" prior to ever sitting down with you. I believe this relationship will be paramount in your decision to hire me as your business coach.

Wright

So who can benefit from having a mindset of Moments of Truth?

Wyatt

I believe every person and organization can benefit. Whether you are the owner, manager, salesperson, or customer service representative, everyone can benefit because it is about the impression that you are leaving on others.

Here is a good example of the importance of customer service: When the market is doing well, most businesses will do well despite their actions. But when times are tough or the market is more competitive, the businesses that are truly adding value and providing exceptional customer service will be the businesses that succeed. Why? Because everyone wants to be treated well, and when we are treated well, we will return to that place of business over and over.

Wright

How about a daily example of a negative and positive Moment of Truth that we can all relate to?

Wyatt

Let's start with the negative experience. About a year ago my family and I moved into a different home, and like many homeowners we have had various repairs and improvements that we needed to make. One of these repairs was in our basement where we were getting water every time it rained. We had five different businesses come and nearly every salesperson spent more time talking about their business than our problem. They asked very few questions, yet were certain that their product or service would solve our problem. Our impression was that they were pushing their product instead of fixing our basement.

For the positive experience I'd like to tell you about a recent car purchase our family made. In the automobile industry there has been a great deal of consolidation of retailers and dealerships. Because of this, there is a lot of competition and many marketing ploys to influence consumers. We have one local dealer who promotes his business as "Your Dealer for Life." The best part is that his actions are congruent with his tagline. The dealership had timely follow-through, the salesman proactively addressed our needs, and he made us feel welcome. It was about us, not about the business. This dealership certainly lives by Moments of Truth and continues to impress us today.

Wright

So what caused you to have a mindset like this and can others do the same?

Wyatt

I believe there are four reasons for my Moments of Truth mindset. The first and biggest reason is my family—not only my parents and my own upbringing, but also the experience my wife and I have had in raising our own children. We teach our children about respect, trust, faith, and quite simply, The Golden Rule, yet these values are just as important in my business. Who wants to do business with someone who is rude or dishonest? I run my business the way I would like to be treated. Try putting on your customer's shoes and seeing your service from their viewpoint.

Secondly, I am always on the lookout for great role models—people who have consistently succeeded. Once I find them, I pay close attention to the characteristics they possess and how they act. I use this information to critique myself and replace those characteristics and actions that are not congruent with my desired image. There are many exceptional role models, locally and globally, that are very successful because of how they treat others.

Third, I am continuously reading books to learn and improve my mindset, my business, and myself. In order to help others, I must improve myself. Teaching others is a huge part of my business as a coach.

Finally, I view a Moment of Truth mindset as a choice. Specifically, it is a choice to provide the highest level of service to everyone I interact with. When we wake up every morning, we have a choice—a choice to make today a great day or a difficult day. I choose to set a new level of expectation and customer service in my business.

Because this mindset is a choice, I believe everyone can live with this mindset. When you make a commitment to have this mindset, and you follow through with the right actions, your customers will experience an incredible level of customer service and they will tell others about you.

Wright

So I guess the next logical question is how do I develop this Moment of Truth mindset?

Wyatt

There are four areas that I believe are critical to developing a Moment of Truth mindset. The first area is to *define and create your brand*. This can be a personal brand or a business brand, but answer the question, "What do I want to be known for?" Your brand should take into account the beliefs you have of yourself or your business.

The second area is *constant learning*. View everything you go through in a day as a lesson or a learning experience. To continually expand your mind, you need to ask yourself, "How can I improve?" or "How can I achieve a different result next time?" You also need to evaluate where you spend your time. Make time every day to work on you. Balance your time doing and your time developing.

In addition, create a list of books you would like to read and make it a goal to read one every week or month. Watch videos, DVDs, or podcasts of seminars or workshops. Constant learning should support the brand we discussed earlier. This is true of your team as well. Everyone on your team should have a developmental plan focused on learning to encourage change and improvements in themselves.

The third area is *preparation*. You cannot create Moments of Truth without preparation. Preparation creates the confidence that you are doing the right things and are performing the way you desire. All areas of your business should be included here. An example of preparation is having processes documented in your business. When you have things documented, you train your team to follow those processes, which creates consistency from the customer's point of view. Consistency is critical in getting return customers.

The fourth area has to do with *eliminating anchors*. An anchor is something that holds you down, just like an anchor on a boat. Anchors can be beliefs that you have about yourself, about the people you work with, or about your customers. You need to identify your own anchors and eliminate them. This might happen by changing your beliefs, changing certain behaviors, or changing the people you spend time with. Stop doing things that are not producing positive fruit. Spend time with people who are going where you are going or have a mindset that matches yours and you will get the results that you want.

In summary, to produce a Moment of Truth mindset you need to define and create your own brand, keep learning, be prepared and have your team prepared, and eliminate anchors that are holding you back.

Wright

What are some specific actions readers can take to achieve the above mindset?

Wyatt

Here are five areas and questions to answer and think about:

1. What do you want to be known for? What impression do you want to leave in every interaction you have on a daily or weekly basis? When you know who you want to be, you know what you are working toward. You must begin with the end in mind. Be specific. Make a list of eleven characteristics or traits that you desire to possess, then begin to develop them.

2. What does your A game look like? Write down in detail how you act, how you are perceived, and how your customer responds to you. Again, be very specific. Get a clear picture of the situation in your mind and write down exactly what it looks like. You are creating a visualization of what you want to be and how you want to act. Once you have visualized it, document it and begin to create and live your A game.

3. When do you want to leave the highest impression? Be very clear and descriptive of those times you *want* to leave the highest impression. In your business, think about what points of client interaction require incredible customer service. Answering your business phone may be one example. Is your phone answered the same way every time? What about when you are in public? Do you (or your team) represent your business in the manner you desire? As a team, agree on what these Moments of Truth look like and when they need to occur. This will wow every customer.

4. How do I change my beliefs to provide the highest level of service possible? Every one of us has beliefs or stories that we tell ourselves daily. In order to change our beliefs we have to eliminate an "I know" mentality where we think we know everything. An "I know" mentality

keeps your mind closed and blocks all learning. Keep your mind open and be willing to learn new things or look at things differently. Your beliefs will not change overnight, but once you identify the beliefs that need to change you can focus on the actions to create that change.

5. How do my behaviors or actions need to change to leave this desired impression? Creating change in behavior is a conscious choice. We must make a decision to either stop or start doing specific actions. What behaviors or actions *need* to change? Need is a very strong word. Dig deep. Be tough on yourself and write down specific behaviors and then focus on making improvements every day. Soon you will create habits in following through on the right actions to deliver your Moments of Truth.

Wright

What final remarks would you like to leave with our audience?

Wyatt

First, I want to recommend that everyone set clear standards for yourself and your business. What are the standards that you and your team are going to play by? Follow those standards and be consistent in every interaction.

Second, make a personal choice to have the passion and desire to develop a Moment of Truth level of customer service. We can choose to change our beliefs and actions. We can choose to leave the highest impression in all interactions.

Third, focus on excellence not perfection. When we focus on perfection we will miss opportunities. Nothing in life is perfect, so define what excellence is and start doing it. Put your ego aside and focus on the customer by asking more questions, listening more clearly, and showing that you care every step of the way.

This is truly what living a Moment of Truth mindset is about. Once you have this mindset, your actions will reflect it and your customers will experience things that they have never experienced before. In competitive times, your business will succeed because you are providing more value and delivering more than what your customers are expecting.

Wright

One last question, I've heard a lot about business coaching and personal coaching lately. How much of business coaching spills over into personal coaching? How does it or how can it help my personal life?

Wyatt

Business coaching includes personal coaching but personal coaching does not always include business coaching. A business will not change until the business owner or manager changes because it starts with the owner's or the manager's beliefs.

For example, let's say a business is not getting enough leads. The business owner or manager may have a strong belief about his or her marketing or message and be unwilling to try new things. I like to say, "If it is working for our competitor, why isn't it working for us?" I believe 80 percent of success in business is in the six inches between a person's ears. Once a person's beliefs are expanded, then the business will begin to expand.

Wright

Well, what a great conversation, Monte. I really appreciate the time you've taken with me today to answer these questions. You have given me a lot to think about. I have learned a lot and I appreciate it.

Wyatt

You are welcome, and I appreciate your time.

Wright

Today we've been talking with Monte Wyatt. Monte helps businesses and business owners bring clarity to how they run and manage their business through his ActionCOACH Business Coaching practice. He helps his clients think through implementation and holds them accountable to the actions and goals to which they commit.

Monte, thank you for being with us today on *Roadmap to Success*.

Wyatt

Thank you, David.

ABOUT THE AUTHOR

As one of the top coaches in ActionCOACH Business Coaching, Monte Wyatt brings over eighteen years of remarkable leadership and personal development experience to businesses and business owners. In addition to coaching clients one-on-one, he conducts pubic and private workshops and seminars. He is a motivational keynote speaker, and a trainer and coach for other business coaches across the United States. Monte is passionate about helping create life abundance for everyone.

Monte Wyatt
ActionCOACH Business Coaching
4117 Walnut Street
West Des Moines, IA 50265
515.222.9193
montewyatt@actioncoach.com
www.coachyourbiz.com or www.actioncoach.com

ROADMAP to SUCCESS 15

An interview with...

Brenda L. Hill-Riggins

David Wright (Wright)

Today we're talking with Brenda L. Hill-Riggins. As the beloved originator of the Royal Collection, Brenda, affectionately known as "the transformation coach," fostered the emergence of an inspirational paradox from an individual perspective and has plans to watch it grow to a billion dollar market. As the driving force behind the success of MARS Contractors, Inc., Brenda is uniquely qualified to talk about success. She is one of America's leading authorities in creating and giving understanding to the transformation process. She is a compelling, empowering, and compassionate coach who has helped many individuals link to and achieve their dreams.

Brenda, welcome to *Roadmap to Success.*

Brenda Hill-Riggins (Hill-Riggins)

Thank you so much for having me.

Wright

So how or what prompted you to begin your journey?

Hill-Riggins

Well, what prompted me to begin my journey and more or less stake my claim to success began after watching the women and men in my community struggle to achieve the American Dream. By my standard, I don't think any of them had accomplished it because I was still hearing a lot of sad stories, and witnessing them as well. I decided I would not end up that way.

To me, the American dream meant owning a house—having that space that you could call home—having the resources to send your children to college, being able to help your family, as well as your community and church. I really didn't see a lot of people in that position and I wanted that. So, I made up my mind to strive and to achieve certain goals in order to be able to assist my family and my community, and not just with material things. (Once I had set my goals and while I was trying to achieve them, I also wanted to experience peace, joy, happiness, and contentment along the way as well.)

After setting goals in order to achieve the things I wanted, I then got busy. I wrote down what I wanted to do, how I wanted to do it, and set some time limits. I allowed the clock to serve as my reference referee in the management of my time. I made a commitment to myself to stay focused.

Wright

So what can one expect to experience on this road to success?

Hill-Riggins

On the road to success there are many wonderful things you can expect to experience. First of all, there is the wonderful opportunity to meet all the other people traveling on that road with you, but you must always remember that they have their own timeframe, and sometimes our time with them is only for an appointed time. We have to know when to let some relationships go and move on. You can expect to experience loneliness, but loneliness can be a good thing. Not very many people make the right choices on a daily basis in order to stay on this particular road; for me it was lonely, but in loneliness I found myself and I was able to have a deeper experience with God.

Wright

You know, I think all of us have heard many, many definitions of success; but tell me, how do you define success?

Hill-Riggins

Well, to me, success is every step that we take, every experience, heartache, and disappointment. Whatever we go through—whether it's positive or negative—is a step toward success. Any experience of change is part of the process of success. If you can understand life's cycles and the different stages of change and where you are in that cycle of change while you're in it, you have gained—you will have prospered and experienced success on some level. Success to me is overstanding what most don't understand. Success is crossing the line from believing to knowing. Success is knowing the only power people have in your life is the power you give them . . . Keep The Power! Success is setting a goal to achieve X and you achieve X, Y, and Z. Success is telling a joke and everybody getting it. Success is going to Antarctica through the Drake Passage and returning home safe. Success is being on safari, a lion starts to charge, then stops. Success is raising children who understand the importance of voting. Success is having a grandchild who sees your accomplishments and asks to be your child. Success is going to your thirtieth class reunion and everyone coming together, holding hands, and praying for a classmate in trouble, a medical crisis. Success knows that *joy* is the essence of God's desire realized. Success is being able to travel this world and see God on the faces of the people, the scenery, animals, and in the beauty of time. Success is making Oprah Winfrey's invitation list—a list I am still working on (smile).

Wright

Did you take a spiritual journey?

Hill-Riggins

My journey has been very, very spiritual because for me, the ultimate success is to know that I'm pleasing God—I know that my actions and reactions are such that they make God smile. I live to make God smile, so yes, it has been a very spiritual journey.

Wright

So what would you say would be the biggest contribution to your professional success?

Hill-Riggins

The biggest contribution to my professional success is the fact that I was able to understand who I am. When you give of yourself it's important to be able to give your authentic self, and you can't do that unless you are in touch with who you really are. Being able to understand who I am, why I am, and what it is I need to do, have all helped me to contribute in a better way. Whether it's family, community, business, or church, I'm able to give totally of myself.

If you understand your purpose and you understand the need you must fill, your ability to give is made easier. How you give and why you give will be at a higher degree of giving—the law of giving will validate your success.

Wright

So aside from your personal role models, who are some of the people who have served as role models for you in the area of success?

Hill-Riggins

The people who have served as role models for me regarding success include Mary, the mother of Jesus. She taught me that success would require a servant's heart. This was a spiritual journey for me, as I explained earlier, so the description of a "virtuous woman" in the book of Proverbs, chapter 31, became a role model for me. It taught me that success would require me to be virtuous. My mother, Cora Hill, taught me that prayer is the key. Oprah Winfrey, the billionaire, taught me that success would require me to be open to receive God's goodness, and giving and having the capability of controlling the airwaves would be a must. Whoopi Goldberg taught me that it is okay for me to be me—to be my authentic self. The comedienne, Adele Givens, taught me that laughter itself will help make the heart glad.

Then there is Lotti Bell Mack, my grandmother, who taught me that happiness is caring for your garden; that's what she loves to do, and that's when she's happy. There's a lady by the name of Vanessa Bell Armstrong, who is a gospel legend (a singer). She taught me that the power of music and song will help heal my spirit.

There is of course Mr. Stephen Covey, and his book, *The 7 Habits of Highly Effective People*, confirmed to me that being kind and caring, and having integrity, honesty, and human dignity would guide me in life. In his book, *Know Can Do!* Ken Blanchard taught me how to make the leap from knowing to doing and gave me the keys to overcoming roadblocks. When I first started reading Stephen Covey's and Ken Blanchard's books, it never occurred to me that one day I would find myself working on a project with them, so I'm really excited about that.

Wright

What do you think are the biggest obstacles people face in trying to become successful?

Hill-Riggins

The biggest obstacle people face is themselves. Most individuals are not aware of the need to change. Every day brings about a change. We must embrace change. Depending on what the obstacle is, we must create a strategy to defeat, conquer, or defend against that obstacle that is holding us back.

Implementing the strategy requires people to become the change they want to see. Not understanding that they need to change, and not doing what they need to do in order to change, are two of the reasons why I say the biggest obstacle people face is themselves. People have goals and dreams but they're not willing to do what they need to do in order to fulfill those dreams. People must become the dream as well as the dream protectors. Do not allow others to kill the dream. The things they need to do require making the right choices, having the right mindset, and knowing when to change, how to change, and why they need to change. These are some of the things I think will help move people forward.

Wright

How do you know what you need to be successful?

Hill-Riggins

Well, for me, I feel that it is in my DNA. I feel that when we were created, what we needed to know to be successful was placed in us; it's like a homing device. For me it is as though I have a GPS—a "God Positioning Satellite"— and the destination is success. (Success in this case is being in sync with God's intent, His desire for my life). Until I understood my purpose, only God knew. What I needed to be successful came to me when the time was right. Success is many different things on many different levels. We already know what we need to do—it's placed in us—but we're not in tune. Sometimes it starts with an awakening—we have to be awakened, reborn, or reconnected, to be able to tap into it. It's not something that you're going to be able to fully grasp all at once and keep to a certain timeline because it is something that is controlled by outside forces of change. It is through my relationship with God that I've been able to strengthen my ability to know. I now think as God intended for me to be, therefore I am.

Wright

Would you tell our readers a little bit about what drives you to be successful?

Hill-Riggins

In my early years, what drove me to be successful were the spirit of competition and the sweet taste of victory. I took competition seriously. I would race my grandchildren and try my hardest to win.

Now that I am a few days older, my main desire is to please God, to be able to encourage my family—especially my children—my grandchildren, and community. I desire to create a level of wealth so my grandchildren can inherit "old money." I want to leave a legacy of faith, honor, and holiness. My goal is to create opportunities for others with no boundaries.

I want to be a compass within a compass. Success is laced with guidelines called rules. One should take the lead (and I'm trying to in my environment) to practice the following things: The Ten Commandments, God's law specifying what we can and cannot do. Then there are the laws of nature involving what we should and should not do. I made a commitment to practice these things and success came to me. Success is a law of nature.

This is America, we can be anything; we can go anywhere. Don't be afraid to test the process—see if it's true. The way I've done that, as I said earlier, is to set a goal, stick to that goal, and do what is right—allowing integrity, honesty, and fairness to guide me and allowing kindness, charity, and compassion to be my only weapons in life. As for me, I can attest to the fact that if you just do these things, there is no way you cannot be successful on every level—mentally, spiritually, physically, educationally, financially, and emotionally.

Wright

Is it important to have balance or to balance the success in your life? If so, how do you balance your success with your life?

Hill-Riggins

It is very important to have balance because peace, which is most important, can only come by way of balance—balance between the mind, body, and spirit. The way I balance success on a day-to-day basis is to first set my goals in every area of my life with a focus on the mind, body, and spirit. The way I'm able to stay on track with those goals is that I make sure to monitor my action plan. I make sure I am feeding my mind by reading, for example. Spiritually, I take time to pray, meditate, or whatever I need to do to stay centered and in sync with God, as well as the universe and the environment. Physically I try to exercise daily.

Balance is very important and the way to achieve it is by staying focused, not just on one area, but in all areas of life, and by being the best you can be.

Wright

What's the message you want people to hear so that they can learn from your success?

Hill-Riggins

The message I want people to hear and learn from my success is this: the one thing people should try to achieve is to understand their purpose in this life. Once they understand that, everything else they need is automatically awakened within them—their hopes, determination, sticktoitiveness, and whatever they may need. I really want people to get this message.

For me, transformation was the key. I had to be awakened to my true potential and to what it was I wanted to do in life, who I wanted to be, and how I wanted to show up for life each day. I want people to be awakened and to know that it is a transformational process they have to go through. If they can understand that, life will not be so difficult. The reason I love to share with others is because it brings understanding. Understanding will eliminate the uncertainties they face from day to day.

Wright

Why do you think more people are not in tune with their passion, if it's something that all people possess?

Hill-Riggins

People are not in tune with their passion because they are not working their purpose. Passion is the spiritual reward for working your purpose. The reason most people are not in tune with our purpose is because we have not asked God what our purpose is. We also know that there will be some work for us to do and sometimes we're just too lazy, therefore we really don't want the "answer" because we don't want to do the work. Also, if our purpose is tied to God, are we ready to be that person that He would have us to be? Are we ready to give up the things we think we might have to give up because of our present day beliefs? Or what we have become accustomed to?

I think people know it's going to take some work and they just don't want to admit they don't want to work.

I simply asked Him one day, "What did you have on your mind when you created me? I know I'm somebody's wife, somebody's mother, and somebody's daughter. But what did you have on your mind when you created me?" The answer was that my purpose was to rekindle God's love for mankind. When I first got that answer, I said, "I will rekindle God's love for mankind. I then thought, "How am I going to be able to do that?"

Wright

All of us probably know what the dictionary definition of passion is, but how do you define it?

Hill-Riggins

Passion is a desire that activates feelings that are linked to a known fact of who you are created to be. Prayer is how passion is communicated to God. Passion is how God's joy is communicated to us. That's what it means to me. I think that's why it's such a great feeling when you finally know your purpose. It's as though you're linked up to the desire that God Himself had when He created you. Passion is the feeling of the desire that God had on His mind about what He desired you to be, whether you were to be a life coach, a transformation coach, care-giver, doctor, or lawyer.

When I understood my purpose laced with my passion, I thought, "Oh my God! So this is what God had on His mind! Wow, that's me, and that's why I feel so passionate when I am speaking, writing, or coaching." I think that when people are linked up to their passion, this is why they say, "You know, if I never made any money from doing this it would be okay because I know why I'm here, I know what I'm supposed to be doing, I'm doing it, and I know it has to please God."

Wright

So what makes your perspective unique?

Hill-Riggins

My perspective on success is unique because I approached success from the perspective of who God created me to be as opposed to who I wanted to be. (www.brendalhill.com). I am a vision surrogate with a unique ability. I remember when I said to God that I wanted to know my purpose, one of the things I said was, "God, please don't let it be a Sunday school teacher. I don't want to be a Sunday school teacher." I knew I was supposed to teach, but I didn't want to be a Sunday school teacher.

One day I received understanding about being a surrogate visionary. People had a tendency to come to me when they felt they needed help if they had a dream or an idea or a vision, and I was always able to help them birth those ideas.

People are searching for their purpose. People don't know it's probably something they're already doing but they're not aware of it. I was already helping people to birth their dreams and their visions. Let me explain.

I have this unique ability to help people birth dreams and visions. It's as though, in a lot of areas within the visuals, there are disconnects within the dream or vision that are making them infertile—an inability to bring forth the idea. For some reason they can't completely conceive the idea. In order to birth it, you've got to first conceive it. So that's where I come in. When they share their dreams or visions with me, I'm able to conceive on their behalf, and help to carry their vision up to a certain point where they are able to birth the vision. I then teach them how to care for the vision. I then give the vision back and they carry it on their own.

The term "surrogate visionary" is new, so let me try to explain. According to the Webster's Unabridged Dictionary, a surrogate is an "artificial or synthetic product that is used as a substitute for a natural product." For me, as a surrogate visionary, this is a good definition to use to explain spiritual manifestations. As a surrogate visionary (Brenda) is an artificial or synthetic visionary that is used as a substitute for a natural visionary (you). Now remember, prayer is: *the act by which the believer communicates with God.*

Actually, a surrogate visionary (Brenda) in a spiritual manifestation is more than just a substitute for a natural visionary (you). In a spiritual manifestation, a surrogate visionary (Brenda) is a necessary generalization—a very close likeness to the natural Created Visionary (you) and is one of the basic elements of spiritual manifestation design.

Let me explain: Every join between dimension levels (*four dimensions of our very own nature—you, mind, body, and spirit*) and fact levels in a spiritual manifestation environment should be based on a surrogate visionary. A surrogate visionary is one who is marked by vision and foresight. This person is someone given to speculation: 1) to meditate on—to reflect, 2) to engage in risky business ventures that offer the chance of large profits, 3) one who has unusual foresight, not as with a natural visionary who has only a mental image produced by the imagination. Understand that a surrogate can extract data logic and systematically look up and replace every incoming idea from the natural visionary with a spiritual equivalent each time either a dimension record (*information gathered from the natural visionary regarding the vision or idea*) or a fact record (*information about the natural visionary's abilities, strengths, and weaknesses*) is brought into the spiritual manifestation environment.

There are still more reasons to use surrogate visionaries. One of the most important is the need to decode uncertain knowledge. If you think carefully about the "I don't know" situations, you may realize that if the right surrogate visionary is used, only one visionary is necessary. Many situations call for a spiritual manifestation through a surrogate visionary. Don't forget that in the spiritual manifestation schema, the visionary must be fertile. A non-fertile visionary automatically turns on the "let's re-examine, re-affirm, re-do, re-think" mode, which is centered around the integrity alarm. The "I don't know" situation occurs quite frequently for years.

Holding on to real vision values (the desire to accomplish via monetary or material worth) as visionaries is also a strategic blunder—not giving birth in just time caused death to the visionary and the vision. Yes, you can navigate through time just as a visionary, thereby avoiding the join with a true surrogate, but you have left most of your opportunity marooned on the natural dimension level. Being a surrogate visionary is new so I try to keep it simpler by saying I am a Transformation Coach. I am now transformed—I am now who God intended me to be—therefore I am a transformation coach.

Wright

Will you explain to our readers how you do what you desire to do?

Hill-Riggins

The way I do what I desire to do is by creating the right structure. First I make sure that my personal foundation is strong. When taking on others' dreams, goals, and wishes, you've got to be very careful that you do not become overwhelmed

So first make sure you have a strong foundation. Second, make sure your infrastructure is strong and make sure you're living what you plan to give.

I had to first make sure that I was up to par mentally, spiritually, emotionally, and financially. I cannot teach what I am not living myself. I want to show up in life each day as a virtuous woman—one who is a woman of her word and can deliver what she says she has to offer. These things had to be in place for me, and that's how I do what I do.

Wright

Well, what an interesting conversation. I really appreciate all this time you've taken with me to talk about this very important subject. It does seem that you have a unique take on success.

Hill-Riggins

I appreciate your having me be a part of this project.

Wright

Today we've been talking with Brenda L. Hill-Riggins, who is affectionately known as "the transformation coach." Brenda is one of America's leading authorities in creating and giving understanding to the transformation process. As we have found out today, I think she knows what she's talking about.

Hill-Riggins

Thank you so much.

Wright

Brenda, thank you being with us today in *Roadmap to Success*.

ABOUT THE AUTHOR

Brenda L. Hill-Riggins is President of MARS Contractors, Inc., a successful family owned and operated construction company. Steered by mother wit and tenacity, Brenda and the team has brought the company a long way in a short period of time. MARS Contractors, Inc. assists with the process, quality, and transference of forces producing and controlling the physical world and its phenomena with the movement of air and water, the essentials for life. MARS Contractors is deeply committed to the best interest of our clients, as well as humanity as a whole. MARS Contractors, Inc. is committed to ensuring complete client satisfaction by delivering quality services through an innovative blend of technology and management expertise.

With a strong desire to help others understand their purpose and move her coaching clients more quickly to their desired destinations in life, in 2007, as an individual, Brenda transitioned from what she does (a contractor) to who she is, a transformation coach. Brenda has given the vision of the company back to her husband, Marcus, to carry. Brenda still oversees and manages the company in the capacity of a business coach.

Brenda completed her speaker's training with The Motivational Center: Dr. Tina Dupree. Brenda completed her coach training at Florida International University: Dr. Martha Beck. Brenda received her Life Coach Certification from the International Coaching Federation and North Star Group. Oprah Winfrey's Life Coach Expert, *New York Times* best-selling author, and *O Magazine* monthly contributor, Dr. Martha Beck, personally trained Brenda. As the beloved originator of The Royal Collection®, Brenda L. Hill-Riggins, affectionately known as "the transformation coach," fostered the emergence of an inspirational understanding from an individual perspective and has plans to watch it grow to a billion dollar market.

Brenda is the mother of four, grandmother of eight. She is a world traveler, loves to cook and entertain, is learning how to be a farmer, and resides in beautiful Miami, Florida, with her husband, Marcus A. Riggins, and their dogs, Bear and Focus.

Brenda L. Hill-Riggins
MARS Contractors, Inc.
www.brendalhill.com